Roberto Clemente

Consulting Editors

Rodolfo Cardona
professor of Spanish
and comparative literature,
Boston University

James Cockcroft
visiting professor of Latin American
and Caribbean studies,
State University of New York at Albany

Hispanics of Achievement

Roberto Clemente

Thomas W. Gilbert

Chelsea House Publishers
New York   Philadelphia

CHELSEA HOUSE PUBLISHERS

Editor-in-Chief: Remmel Nunn
Managing Editor: Karyn Gullen Browne
Copy Chief: Juliann Barbato
Picture Editor: Adrian G. Allen
Art Director: Maria Epes
Deputy Copy Chief: Mark Rifkin
Assistant Art Director: Noreen Romano
Manufacturing Manager: Gerald Levine
Systems Manager: Lindsey Ottman
Production Manager: Joseph Romano
Production Coordinator: Marie Claire Cebrián

Hispanics of Achievement
Senior Editor: John W. Selfridge

Staff for ROBERTO CLEMENTE
Associate Editor: Philip Koslow
Copy Editor: Brian Sookram
Editorial Assistant: Martin Mooney
Picture Researcher: Alan Gottlieb
Cover Illustration: Patti Oleon

3 5 7 9 8 6 4 2

Library of Congress Cataloging-in-Publication Data
Gilbert, Tom
   Roberto Clemente/Tom Gilbert
      p. cm.—(Hispanics of achievement)
   Includes bibliographical references and index.
   Summary: Biography of the Hall of Fame baseball player from
Puerto Rico.
   ISBN 0-7910-1240-9
        0-7910-1267-0 (pbk.)
   1. Clemente, Roberto, 1934–72—Juvenile literature. 2. Baseball
players—Biography—Juvenile literature. 3. Hispanic Americans—
Biography—Juvenile literature.[1. Clemente, Roberto, 1934–72.
2. Baseball players 3. Hispanic Americans—Biography.]
I. Title II. Series
GV865.C45G55 1991
92—dc20   90-44690
[796.357'092]   CIP
[B]   AC

Contents

Hispanics of Achievement

Oscar Arias Sánchez
Costa Rican president

Joan Baez
Mexican-American folksinger

Rubén Blades
Panamanian lawyer and entertainer

Jorge Luis Borges
Argentine writer

Juan Carlos
king of Spain

Pablo Casals
Spanish cellist and conductor

Miguel de Cervantes
Spanish writer

Cesar Chavez
Mexican-American labor leader

El Cid
Spanish military leader

Roberto Clemente
Puerto Rican baseball player

Plácido Domingo
Spanish singer

El Greco
Spanish artist

Gloria Estefan
Cuban-American singer

Gabriel García Márquez
Colombian writer

Raul Julia
Puerto Rican actor

Diego Maradona
Argentine soccer player

José Martí
Cuban revolutionary and poet

Rita Moreno
Puerto Rican singer and actress

Pablo Neruda
Chilean poet and diplomat

Antonia Novello
U.S. surgeon general

Octavio Paz
Mexican poet and critic

Javier Pérez de Cuéllar
Peruvian diplomat

Anthony Quinn
Mexican-American actor

Diego Rivera
Mexican artist

Antonio López de Santa Anna
Mexican general and politician

George Santayana
Spanish poet and philosopher

Junípero Serra
Spanish missionary and explorer

Lee Trevino
Mexican-American golfer

Pancho Villa
Mexican revolutionary

CHELSEA HOUSE PUBLISHERS

INTRODUCTION

Hispanics of Achievement

Rodolfo Cardona

The Spanish language and many other elements of Spanish culture are present in the United States today and have been since the
country's earliest beginnings. Some of these elements have come
directly from the Iberian Peninsula; others have come indirectly, by
way of Mexico, the Caribbean basin, and the countries of Central
and South America.

Spanish culture has influenced America in many subtle ways,
and consequently many Americans remain relatively unaware of
the extent of its impact. The vast majority of them recognize the
influence of Spanish culture in America, but they often do not
realize the great importance and long history of that influence.
This is partly because Americans have tended to judge the Hispanic
influence in the United States in statistical terms rather than
to look closely at the ways in which individual Hispanics have
profoundly affected American culture. For this reason, it is fitting

that Americans obtain more than a passing acquaintance with the origins of these Spanish cultural elements and gain an understanding of how they have been woven into the fabric of American society.

It is well documented that Spanish seafarers were the first to explore and colonize many of the early territories of what is today called the United States of America. For this reason, students of geography discover Hispanic names all over the map of the United States. For instance, the Strait of Juan de Fuca was named after the Spanish explorer who first navigated the waters of the Pacific Northwest; the names of states such as Arizona (arid zone), Montana (mountain), Florida (thus named because it was reached on Easter Sunday, which in Spanish is called the feast of Pascua Florida), and California (named after a fictitious land in one of the first and probably the most popular among the Spanish novels of chivalry, *Amadis of Gaul*) are all derived from Spanish; and there are numerous mountains, rivers, canyons, towns, and cities with Spanish names throughout the United States.

Not only explorers but many other illustrious figures in Spanish history have helped define American culture. For example, the 13th-century king of Spain, Alfonso X, also known as the Learned, may be unknown to the majority of Americans, but his work on the codification of Spanish law has greatly influenced the evolution of American law, particularly in the jurisdictions of the Southwest. For this contribution a statue of him stands in the rotunda of the Capitol in Washington, D.C. Likewise, the name Diego Rivera may be unfamiliar to most Americans, but this Mexican painter influenced many American artists whose paintings, commissioned during the Great Depression and the New Deal era of the 1930s, adorn the walls of government buildings throughout the United States. In recent years the contributions of Puerto Ricans, Mexicans, Mexican Americans (Chicanos), and Cubans in American cities such as Boston, Chicago, Los Angeles,

Miami, Minneapolis, New York, and San Antonio have been enormous.

The importance of the Spanish language in this vast cultural complex cannot be overstated. Spanish, after all, is second only to English as the most widely spoken of Western languages within the United States as well as in the entire world. The popularity of the Spanish language in America has a long history.

In addition to Spanish exploration of the New World, the great Spanish literary tradition served as a vehicle for bringing the language and culture to America. Interest in Spanish literature in America began when English immigrants brought with them translations of Spanish masterpieces of the Golden Age. As early as 1683, private libraries in Philadelphia and Boston contained copies of the first picaresque novel, *Lazarillo de Tormes*, translations of Francisco de Quevedo's *Los Sueños*, and copies of the immortal epic of reality and illusion *Don Quixote*, by the great Spanish writer Miguel de Cervantes. It would not be surprising if Cotton Mather, the arch-Puritan, read *Don Quixote* in its original Spanish, if only to enrich his vocabulary in preparation for his writing *La fe del cristiano en 24 artículos de la Institución de Cristo, enviada a los españoles para que abran sus ojos* (The Christian's Faith in 24 Articles of the Institution of Christ, Sent to the Spaniards to Open Their Eyes), published in Boston in 1699.

Over the years, Spanish authors and their works have had a vast influence on American literature—from Washington Irving, John Steinbeck, and Ernest Hemingway in the novel to Henry Wadsworth Longfellow and Archibald MacLeish in poetry. Such important American writers as James Fenimore Cooper, Edgar Allan Poe, Walt Whitman, Mark Twain, and Herman Melville all owe a sizable debt to the Spanish literary tradition. Some writers, such as Willa Cather and Maxwell Anderson, who explored Spanish themes they came into contact with in the American Southwest and Mexico, were influenced less directly but no less profoundly.

Important contributions to a knowledge of Spanish culture in the United States were also made by many lesser known individuals—teachers, publishers, historians, entrepreneurs, and others—with a love for Spanish culture. One of the most significant of these contributions was made by Abiel Smith, a Harvard College graduate of the class of 1764, when he bequeathed stock worth $20,000 to Harvard for the support of a professor of French and Spanish. By 1819 this endowment had produced enough income to appoint a professor, and the philologist and humanist George Ticknor became the first holder of the Abiel Smith Chair, which was the very first endowed Chair at Harvard University. Other illustrious holders of the Smith Chair would include the poets Henry Wadsworth Longfellow and James Russell Lowell.

A highly respected teacher and scholar, Ticknor was also a collector of Spanish books, and as such he made a very special contribution to America's knowledge of Spanish culture. He was instrumental in amassing for Harvard libraries one of the first and most impressive collections of Spanish books in the United States. He also had a valuable personal collection of Spanish books and manuscripts, which he bequeathed to the Boston Public Library.

With the creation of the Abiel Smith Chair, Spanish language and literature courses became part of the curriculum at Harvard, which also went on to become the first American university to offer graduate studies in Romance languages. Other colleges and universities throughout the United States gradually followed Harvard's example, and today Spanish language and culture may be studied at most American institutions of higher learning.

No discussion of the Spanish influence in the United States, however brief, would be complete without a mention of the Spanish influence on art. Important American artists such as John Singer Sargent, James A. M. Whistler, Thomas Eakins, and Mary Cassatt all explored Spanish subjects and experimented with Spanish techniques. Virtually every serious American artist living today has studied the work of the Spanish masters as well as the great 20th-century Spanish painters Salvador Dalí, Joan Miró, and Pablo Picasso.

The most pervasive Spanish influence in America, however, has probably been in music. Compositions such as Leonard Bernstein's *West Side Story*, the Latinization of William Shakespeare's *Romeo and Juliet* set in New York's Puerto Rican quarter, and Aaron Copland's *Salon Mexico* are two obvious examples. In general, one can hear the influence of Latin rhythms—from tango to mambo, from guaracha to salsa—in virtually every form of American music.

This series of biographies, which Chelsea House has published under the general title HISPANICS OF ACHIEVEMENT, constitutes further recognition of—and a renewed effort to bring forth to the consciousness of America's young people—the contributions that Hispanic people have made not only in the United States but throughout the civilized world. The men and women who are featured in this series have attained a high level of accomplishment in their respective fields of endeavor and have made a permanent mark on American society.

The title of this series must be understood in its broadest possible sense: The term *Hispanics* is intended to include Spaniards, Spanish Americans, and individuals from many countries whose language and culture have either direct or indirect Spanish origins. The names of many of the people included in this series will be immediately familiar; others will be less recognizable. All, however, have attained recognition within their own countries, and often their fame has transcended their borders.

The series HISPANICS OF ACHIEVEMENT thus addresses the attainments and struggles of Hispanic people in the United States and seeks to tell the stories of individuals whose personal and professional lives in some way reflect the larger Hispanic experience. These stories are exemplary of what human beings can accomplish, often against daunting odds and by extraordinary personal sacrifice, where there is conviction and determination.

Fray Junípero Serra, the 18th-century Spanish Franciscan missionary, is one such individual. Although in very poor health, he devoted the last 15 years of his life to the foundation of missions throughout California—then a mostly unsettled expanse of land—in an effort to bring a better life to Native Americans through the cultivation of crafts and animal husbandry. An example from recent times, the Mexican-American labor leader Cesar Chavez has battled bitter opposition and made untold personal sacrifices in his effort to help poor agricultural workers who have been exploited for decades on farms throughout the Southwest.

The talent with which each one of these men and women may have been endowed required dedication and hard work to develop and become fully realized. Many of them have enjoyed rewards for their efforts during their own lifetime, whereas others have died poor and unrecognized. For some it took a long time to achieve their goals, for others success came at an early age, and for still others the struggle continues. All of them, however, stand out as people whose lives have made a difference, whose achievements we need to recognize today and should continue to honor in the future.

Roberto Clemente

Poised and ready in the batter's box, Roberto Clemente shows the intensity and concentration that he maintained throughout his 18 seasons in the major leagues. Clemente's performance in the 1971 World Series established him as one of baseball's superstars.

CHAPTER ONE

Center Stage

Roberto Clemente stood on the lush green infield of Baltimore's Memorial Stadium, listening to the last notes of the national anthem and awaiting the opening of the 1971 World Series. Looking around the double-decked ballpark, he saw thousands of Orioles fans and hundreds of pro-Orioles banners; everything that could be painted, printed, or dyed seemed to be orange and black, the colors of the American League champion Baltimore Orioles. It reminded Clemente how sick and tired he was of hearing that his team, the National League champion Pittsburgh Pirates, did not have a chance in the best-of-seven-games series. One of the morning's newspapers gave the Pirates the same odds as General Custer had at the Battle of the Little Bighorn; another jokingly predicted, "the Orioles in three games." And to top everything off, when he took a taxi from the hotel to the ballpark, Clemente had found himself riding with one of the loudest Orioles fans in Baltimore. As he later recalled, "The cab driver began telling me how much better the Orioles were than the Pirates. I knew he didn't know what he was talking about, but I started arguing with him anyway. Don't ask me why, but I did."

If the cabdriver had known anything about Roberto Clemente's character, he would have kept quiet. Adversity—whether it came in the form of a physical injury, criticism, or someone telling him that a thing could not be done—did not discourage Clemente; it only made him play better. Opposing National League managers had learned over the years that the best strategy against Clemente was, as one put it, to "let him sleep."

Going into the 1971 World Series, sleep was something Clemente never seemed to be able to get enough of. The daily grind of the season and the pennant race had left him exhausted. He had turned 37 in August and was completing his 17th major league season. He had played in 2,329 National League games and come to bat 9,076 times, more than any other player in the 84-year history of the Pittsburgh Pirates and more than all but a few dozen men in the history of the major leagues.

Unlike most of those men, however, Clemente did not usually take the winter off. Along with many Puerto Rican, Dominican, and other Hispanic ballplayers, he felt an obligation to perform in the winter leagues for the people back home, who could only see big-league baseball on television, if at all. As Clemente once observed, with a touch of exaggeration: "A ten-year period in the major leagues is considered a long career, right? Well, I have played 18 years here and 14 years in the Winter League. Thirty two seasons, that's three careers." Adding in the games Clemente had played in the winter, by 1971 he had already appeared in more than 2,800 games and come to bat almost 11,000 times since his rookie season in 1955. Only St. Louis Cardinal Hall of Famer Stan Musial and the great Ty Cobb, who played 24 years and batted .367—the highest career batting mark ever—had seen as much action during their big-league careers.

Roberto Clemente had something else in common with Ty Cobb, whose Detroit Tigers won only 3 pennants during his 22

Clemente leaps high against the fence in pursuit of a long fly ball during the 1971 National League playoffs. Several times during his career, Clemente injured himself by crashing into outfield fences. As he told a reporter during the World Series, "I gave everything I had to this game."

years with the team, and none at all when Cobb was in his prime. Clemente had toiled most of his career for a noncontending team.

Comparing the Pirates' record during the late 1960s and early 1970s to that of the Orioles, it is not surprising that Clemente and his team were rated such underdogs in the 1971 World Series. After winning their first National League flag in 33 years in 1960, Pittsburgh had struggled through the entire next decade, losing almost as many games as they won; they never finished better than third place in the standings. They revived in 1970, when Willie Stargell hit 31 home runs and Clemente batted .352 through September, when his season was cut short by a sprained back. Led by these two, the Pirates won the Eastern Division of the National League, only to be humiliated in the best-of-five-games pennant playoffs, when they lost three straight games to the Cincinnati Reds, who were aptly nicknamed the Big Red Machine.

The Pirates bounced back in 1971, when an even better season from Stargell, who swatted 48 homers and drove in 125 runs, propelled them to another Eastern Division championship. The Pirates went on to upset the San Francisco Giants, three games to one, to win the pennant. (Clemente batted .333 with 4 RBIs in the playoffs, while ace reliever Dave Giusti saved all 3 Pittsburgh victories without yielding an earned run.) But still the Pirates made few believers.

The Pirates' detractors had only to point to the Baltimore Orioles, a team that deserved to be ranked with the best in modern baseball history. After winning the American League pennant and the World Series in 1966 and finishing second in 1968, the Orioles won their division in 1969, 1970, and 1971, averaging 106 wins and only 56 losses a season. They had been near-perfect in postseason play, winning all three playoff series in three-game sweeps and taking the 1970 World Series from the Reds in five games. The only blemish on their October record was the 1969 World Series loss to the New York Mets, but this was widely dismissed as a fluke.

The 1971 edition may have been the best Baltimore team of all. Managed brilliantly by Earl Weaver, the Orioles featured slugger Frank Robinson, who already had 500 home runs to his credit, and a state-of-the-art defense featuring Mark Belanger at shortstop, Brooks Robinson at third base, and Paul Blair in center field. The four-man rotation of Dave McNally, Pat Dobson, Mike Cuellar, and Jim Palmer was the only staff in baseball history, other than the 1920 Chicago White Sox, to have four 20-game winners. Not surprisingly, the odds makers had Baltimore as heavy 9–5 favorites to win the 1971 World Series. Even the Japanese were betting on the Orioles. Before a single game had been played, the Japanese baseball leagues invited the expected champs for a post–World Series tour of their country. An irritated Pirates manager Danny

Murtaugh commented, "After what I read and hear, I wonder why we even bothered to show up."

If the 1971 World Series was a challenge for the Pirates as a team, it was just as great a challenge for Roberto Clemente personally. In a way, he was an underdog too. In spite of his .318 lifetime batting average, 4 National League batting titles, a dozen Gold Glove Awards for fielding excellence, and other individual honors, Clemente was not widely recognized as a superstar outside the city limits of Pittsburgh, Pennsylvania. This was largely because he had never had much of an opportunity to show what he could do on baseball's national stage, the playoffs and the World Series. In the 1960 World Series, when the Pirates upset the New York Yankees, the young Clemente had been overshadowed by veteran stars such as Dick Groat and Don Hoak. Now, although still an all-star and a respected team leader, he was past his peak physically and beginning to be eclipsed by younger players such as Stargell and catcher Manny Sanguillen. Baseball history is full of great stars who were forever underrated because they never got a chance to shine in October, when all the nation's fans are watching. In October 1971, it looked as though Roberto Clemente was destined to be one of them.

When the 1971 World Series got under way before 53,000 fans in Memorial Stadium, things went well enough for the Pirates. They opened the scoring in the second inning of Game 1 with three unearned runs on errors by Belanger and catcher Elrod Hendricks. But the Pirates starting pitcher Dock Ellis, hampered by a sore elbow, could not hold the Orioles in check. Don Buford, Merv Rettenmund, and Frank Robinson each homered, and Dave McNally struck out nine and walked only two over nine innings. The Orioles won, 5–3. Game 2, which was postponed a day by rain, was more of the same; the Orioles hitters roughed up 6 Pittsburgh pitchers for 14 hits and gave Jim Palmer an 11–0 lead by the sixth inning; the final score was 11–3. Baseball's newspaper pundits were delighted to see all their predictions of a one-sided series coming

Pirates slugger Willie Stargell (8) heads disgustedly back to the dugout after striking out with two men on base during Game 2 of the 1971 World Series. Stargell was mired in a slump throughout the series, but Clemente's torrid hitting sparked the Pirates to victory.

true. One crowed, "The World Series is no longer a contest. It's an atrocity; it's the Germans marching through Belgium."

The Pittsburgh Pirates may have had few believers, but they still had Roberto Clemente. In the first game, Clemente had doubled and singled for two of his team's three hits. He went two-for-five in the next game, including another double, to bring his World Series record to four-for-nine; up to this point no other Pirate had more than one hit. On defense, Clemente put the Orioles on notice that they were not to take any liberties on the base paths. The Orioles were staging a game-breaking six-run rally in the bottom of the fifth inning of Game 2. Speedy Merv Rettenmund stood on second with Frank Robinson at bat. Robinson hit a drive to right field that appeared to be deep enough to allow Rettenmund to tag up and advance to third. Clemente caught the ball on the run, whirled, and threw it to third base on the fly. The ball traveled more than 300 feet in the air and came within inches of beating the runner to the base. No one in the crowd could believe that he had even made it close. After the game, an Orioles player called it the "greatest throw I ever saw"; Roberto Clemente's teammates, of course, had seen better.

After Game 2, the series moved to Pittsburgh's brand-new Three Rivers Stadium—also known as the House That Clemente Built—for the next three games. The Orioles already knew how dangerous Clemente could be with his bat, his glove, and his arm. They were about to find out that Clemente could also beat them with his legs.

Pittsburgh got to Cuellar early in Game 3, with one out in the opening inning. With men on first and third, Clemente hit a potential double-play ground ball but beat the relay to first base, allowing the runner on third to score. The two starters duelled until the bottom of the seventh, when Clemente led off, with the score 2–1 in the Pirates' favor. He topped an easy roller back to the mound that Cuellar fielded a little casually. Suddenly, Cuellar looked up to see Clemente hustling down the line at full speed; he panicked and threw wide of the base, allowing Clemente to reach safely. Visibly rattled, Cuellar then walked Willie Stargell and hung a screwball that slugger Bob Robertson drove over the left-field fence. Pittsburgh won, 5–1.

Even though Baltimore held a 2–1 lead in games, *New York Daily News* columnist Dick Young had already seen enough to make up his mind about who was the dominant player in the series. Referring to the Dodge Charger that was to be given by *Sport* magazine to the World Series Most Valuable Player, Young wrote, "The best damn ballplayer in the World Series, maybe in the whole world, is Roberto Clemente, and as far as I'm concerned they can give him the automobile right now."

Clemente and the Pirates kept right on rolling, winning Game 4 by a score of 4–3 on reliever Bruce Kison's 6⅓-inning, one-hit performance, then shutting out the Orioles 4–0 behind Nelson Briles's complete-game two-hitter.

Game 4 was special because it was the first World Series game ever to be played at night. Regular-season night baseball had been tried first in Cincinnati in the late 1930s, before the coming of television; in the 1940s and 1950s it became very popular with the millions of fans who worked during the day. Still, tradition dictated that the World Series be played in the sunshine. By 1970, however, more than 90 percent of American homes had television, and TV contracts were paying an ever-increasing share of baseball's way. Under pressure to improve the World Series TV ratings in 1971, Commissioner Bowie Kuhn scheduled Game 4 at night as an experiment.

The experiment was a huge success. Sixty-one million people tuned in that Thursday evening, dwarfing the record Three Rivers crowd of 51,378. According to NBC, which was carrying the series, the game appeared on half of the TV sets in the country and attracted the largest prime-time audience of any sporting event in history.

It did not take long for Roberto Clemente to grab center stage. Coming to bat in the third inning with one out and Richie Hebner on first base, Clemente created the kind of drama and emotion that television cameras love. Orioles right-hander Pat Dobson aimed a pitch at the low outside corner of the plate, but he left the ball within striking distance of Clemente's sweeping swing. Clemente promptly lined a shot into the right-field corner, right at the foul line. It looked like a home run, but umpire John Rice spread his arms to signal a foul ball. Clemente's home run trot turned into an angry sprint down the right-field line toward Rice; he was met there by first base coach Don Leppert and Pirates manager Danny Murtaugh, all three of them bitterly protesting the call. The television audience was treated to a five-minute miniriot, interrupted by replays proving that the ball had, in truth, gone foul by inches. After composing himself, Clemente rapped a hard single that put Hebner in position to score on Al Oliver's base hit.

Clemente singled to center in the fifth inning and beat out an infield grounder in the eighth for his third hit of the evening.

He added an RBI single the next day in Game 5, which the Pirates won by a score of 4–0. People began to notice that he had got at least 1 hit in each of his 12 career World Series games, going back to 1960. A search of the record books turned up only 1 longer World Series hitting streak, 17 games by Yankee outfielder Hank Bauer during the 1956, 1957, and 1958 series. But only Roberto Clemente had hit safely in every World Series game he had played in.

There was another streak going in the 1971 World Series, one that the Pirates hoped to break as they traveled back to Baltimore for Games 6 and 7—so far the home team had won every game. The Orioles drew little comfort from this; weighing heavily on their mind was the thought that if they lost Game 6, they would go down in history as the only team ever to win the first two games of a World Series and then lose the next four straight. So in pregame batting practice, Baltimore's Brooks Robinson was surprised to see a player wearing the black-and-gold-trimmed uniform of the Pirates suffering from what looked like a case of nerves. It was Clemente. "He was storming around the batting cage," Robinson said later, "ranting about what he had to do to prove what kind of hitter he is."

Clemente was fuming about an article that had appeared in a Baltimore paper the day before, saying that his bat was no longer quick enough to pull the ball and criticizing him for not hitting with more power. Clemente's reaction was predictable. With two out in the first inning, he stepped up to the plate against Jim Palmer and lined a high fastball off the left-center-field wall for a triple. In his next at-bat, he homered to right to make it 2–0 Pittsburgh. Four Pirates pitchers eventually squandered the lead, and the Orioles won the game 3–2 on Brooks Robinson's sacrifice fly in the 10th. But it would have ended in nine if not for another amazing throw by Clemente that froze the potential winning run at third base. "It had to be the greatest throw I've ever seen," said Baltimore second baseman Davey Johnson, who was watching from the on-deck circle. "One moment he's got his back to the plate at the 309-foot mark and the next instant here comes the throw, on the chalk line."

Now tied at three games apiece, the World Series came down to a matchup between Pittsburgh's Steve Blass and Baltimore's Mike Cuellar. But regardless of the outcome, Roberto Clemente had already put his stamp on the series. In the words of Roger Angell, covering the series for *New Yorker* magazine, it was "a kind of baseball that none of us had ever seen before—throwing and running and hitting at something close to the level of absolute perfection, playing to win but also playing the game as if it were a form of punishment for everyone else on the field." Clemente knew that he had made his point. As he told Angell before the seventh game, "I want everybody in the world to know that this is the way I play all the time. All season, every season. I gave everything I had to this game."

Blass threw a complete-game four-hitter, outpitching Cuellar to make the Pirates world champions by a score of 2–1. Again Clemente supplied the drama, in the top of the fourth inning: Delivering one last message to the Orioles, Baltimore cab-drivers, and sportswriters who didn't appreciate his swing, he powered Cuellar's first pitch over the 360-foot mark in left-center field, tying the score at 1–1.

After the game, the winning locker room was a scene of absolute pandemonium, as the joyful Pirates celebrated amid a tangle of electrical cables, glaring TV lights, and the general bustle of hundreds of reporters at work. "I can't believe it! I can't believe it!" shouted Blass. Sitting pensively in front of his locker, Clemente declined to join in the horseplay. "Oh," he said, "that's o.k. for the younger fellows."

Clemente's 1971 World Series statistics are startling—a .414 batting average, .759 slugging average, and at least 1 hit in each of the 7 games. His 12 hits, including 2 home runs, a triple, and 2 doubles, were the most by any hitter on either team. He recorded

With the Pirates trailing 1–0 in the fourth inning of Game 7, Clemente jumped on Mike Cuellar's first pitch and drove the ball over the 360-foot mark in left field to tie the score. Jose Pagan's RBI double provided the winning margin for the Pirates as Steve Blass blanked the Orioles the rest of the way.

no outfield assists, and for a good reason. After his throw in Game 2, not a single Baltimore runner tried to take an extra base on him.

However, the numbers alone fail to indicate what Clemente's leadership meant to his team. As Willie Stargell later wrote, "Roberto kept our fighting spirit finely tuned. He was a fierce competitor . . . . He was also the finest all-around player in the major leagues at the time. . . . Each one of us wanted to be like Roberto. He taught us to take pride in ourselves, our team and our profession."

When Roberto Clemente finally stepped in front of the microphones to accept his Most Valuable Player Award, he did not talk about himself. His thoughts were with his family back home in Puerto Rico, who were watching on television. "Before I say anything, I want to say something in Spanish to my mother and father," he said in a calm, low voice. *"En este, el momento más grande de mi vida, les pido la bendición"*—"At this, the greatest moment of my life, I ask your blessing."

A house in a sugar mill village in Puerto Rico, photographed in 1942. In the town of Carolina, where Clemente was born, there was little work apart from harvesting sugarcane. "I grew up with people who really had to struggle to eat," he recalled.

CHAPTER TWO

"Earn It"

Roberto Clemente's parents, Melchor and Luisa Clemente, watched the 1971 World Series from the comfortable house that their son had bought for them in a neat suburban neighborhood of San Juan, the capital of Puerto Rico. But on August 18, 1934, when Roberto Walker Clemente was born, the family lived in a very different place. In those days, Roberto, his sister, three brothers, and Luisa's son and daughter by a previous marriage all shared a wooden frame house in a rural *barrio*—the Spanish term for "neighborhood" or "quarter"—called San Antón, not far from where Melchor and Luisa Clemente had themselves been born and raised. San Antón was part of the town of Carolina, which is now a busy industrial sector but was then made up mostly of acres and acres of densely planted sugarcane. Like most of his neighbors and their fathers before them, Melchor Clemente supported his family by working in the fields.

Requiring a unique combination of strength, stamina, and precision, the harvesting of sugarcane by hand is one of the world's most arduous jobs. Melchor Clemente and his fellow workers would begin the harvest in late fall, when the 10- to 15-foot cane stalks are crowned by silky, whitish flowers. The workers formed large crews and spent from sunup to early evening in the fields, swinging long, curved knives called machetes back and forth as they mowed down row after row of cane. Typically, they stopped only to eat two hearty meals of rice and beans, chicken, plantains, and salad that their wives or children brought out to them in *fiambreras*, metal containers with several compartments. The work, which continued through the winter months, was very hard on the back and arms, and it gave those who did it lean, wiry builds and distinctively overdeveloped lower back muscles. Because the cane had to be severed cleanly and as close as possible to the ground in order not to waste the sugary juice, the cane cutters spent most of the day stooped forward at the waist. The work was dirty, and to guard against the black, sticky grime that was left over from the yearly field burnings, the cane cutters had to wear heavy clothing and boots, no matter how warm the weather. Even at Christmastime, the Puerto Rican sun can be brutally hot.

Melchor Clemente's job was also dangerous. The men worked side by side and close together, and their three- to four-foot-long machetes were as sharp as razors; thus any misstep or break in the rhythm of the group could result in a badly cut arm or leg. A further danger came from bites, rashes, and infections inflicted by the insects and disease-carrying bacteria residing in the wet, spongy soil that sugarcane favors.

Many years later, whenever Roberto Clemente the professional ballplayer was feeling worn out, he would recall the sight of his father and the others sweating in the cane fields. "Just think of all those people," he would say, "waking up so early in the morning, cutting cane in the hot sun. How can I feel tired if all I have to do is play baseball?"

San Antón was a poor community, even before the economic depression of the 1930s and World War II, which took an even

Workers cut sugarcane in Puerto Rico during the 1940s. Melchor Clemente, Roberto's father, worked long hours in the cane fields to support his family. Remembering his father's backbreaking labor, Clemente later asked, "How can I feel tired if all I have to do is play baseball?"

greater toll on Puerto Rico than on the rest of the United States. Money and food were scarce, and most people lived without amenities like indoor plumbing and good medical care. Luisa Clemente's children were delivered by midwives instead of doctors, and the infant mortality rate in rural areas was high; Roberto's sister, Ana Iris, died when she was five, and his older half sister, Rosa María, died while giving birth. Still, relatively, the Clementes were not badly off. Melchor Clemente worked extra hours, running a small food business and making deliveries with his truck, to make sure that none of his children went hungry. To Roberto Clemente, his childhood may have been poor, but it was happy and secure. As he later said, "I was so happy, because my brothers and my father and my mother, we used to get together at night, and we used to sit down and make jokes, and we used to eat whatever we had to eat. And this was something wonderful to me. I grew up with people who really had to struggle to eat. During the war, when food was hard to get, my parents fed their children first and they took what was left. They always thought of us."

The Clementes were affectionate with their children, but they also stressed the values of education and discipline. Luisa Clemente sent her children to the local elementary school and urged all of them, with varying degrees of success, to continue with their education. Young Roberto idolized his father, who provided him with a living example of self-sacrifice and the dignity of physical labor. Clemente recalled that his father used to say, "I want you to be a good man, I want you to work, and I want you to be a serious person." As a child, Roberto liked to accompany his father to work, where he received an education in the hard facts of life. When the boss's fancy car drove down the dusty dirt roads that ran along the sugarcane fields, Melchor Clemente would often point to the man riding inside and remind his son, "He is no better than you."

Roberto learned his lessons well. When he was nine years old, he asked his father for a bicycle. The answer he got was, "Earn it." Soon, Roberto found a job lugging a heavy metal milk can the half mile each way from a neighbor's house to a local general store for a few pennies a day. "Six o'clock every morning, I went for the milk," the adult Roberto Clemente remembered. "I wanted to do it. I wanted to have work. . . . I grew up with that in mind. Maybe that is why I don't smile so often." It took him 3 years to save up the $27 for the used bicycle, but he stuck with it.

Friends and relatives considered Roberto a quiet, respectful boy. His mother remembered Roberto always asking for *la bendición,* his parents' blessing. This is a traditional Spanish expression by which a person pays respect to a parent or other elder. The meaning behind it is to show humility by figuratively placing the other person between oneself and God. It is a custom that has virtually disappeared among young people in Puerto Rico today. According to Roberto's 10th-grade history teacher, Mrs. Cáceres, he had a shy and soft-spoken demeanor in school as well and always answered questions with his eyes fixed on the classroom floor. She was struck less by his schoolwork than by his already amazing running speed and a pair of big hands that, as she said, "would express what he could not say in words."

Clemente's hands turned out to be only one of many attributes that emerged when the young Roberto fell in love with baseball, which had been an integral part of Puerto Rican culture and tradition since the 19th century. He consciously developed his hands for the game by always carrying around a rubber ball. "I squeezed it to strengthen my fingers and wrists and my friend and I would walk to and from school throwing the rubber ball back and forth," Clemente explained later. "Many times at night, I lay in bed and threw the ball against the ceiling and caught it. Baseball was my whole life." Early on, he sensed that he had a special gift and was destined to become a ballplayer. "I became convinced," he said, "[that] God wanted me to. I was sure I came to this world for a reason."

Kept up at night by the noise of Roberto's bouncing rubber ball and annoyed when local sandlot games would make him late for mealtimes, Luisa Clemente became less and less patient with her son's passion. This was particularly true on Sundays, when all the Clemente children would wear their finest white clothing: "Sometimes I'd dress him up nice and clean, and he'd come home full of dust and mud! I'd send him to the store on an errand and he'd be gone for hours!" Finally, she decided on a punishment. As Roberto Clemente told the story, "She started to burn my bat, but I got it out of the fire and saved it. Many times [now] she tells me how wrong she was and how right I was to want to play baseball. I bought my parents their home in Puerto Rico and gave them possessions they thought they'd never see. All from baseball." Years later, Clemente still liked to tease his mother affectionately by saying that he had inherited his famous strong arm from her. "I got my good arm from my mother," he deadpanned in a 1964 interview. "Today she's 73, yet she can throw a ball from second base to home plate with something on it!"

Melchor Clemente was more tolerant, especially when he saw what his son could do on the baseball diamond. (Once, Roberto hit 10 home runs in a San Antón sandlot game.) Sometimes, Clemente's father sent him on errands that took him into San Juan proper and past Sixto Escobar Stadium, where the Puerto Rican League San Juan Senadores (Senators) played. Situated on a plot of sandy ground near El Escambrón beach and only partially sheltered from the constant sea breezes by a stand of tall pines, Sixto Escobar was an old ballpark with extremely small outfield dimensions. (It has since been replaced by the more modern Hiram Bithorn Stadium.) But for Roberto Clemente, it was paradise. There, in awe, he watched for the first time the smooth brand of baseball played by professionals. He became so attached to Senadores outfielder Monte Irvin, the great Negro League slugger who later played for the National League New York Giants, that the boys he played with in the pickup games of San Antón began to call him "Monte Irvin."

One day, when Roberto was 14 years old, he and his friends were playing on a sandlot, using a stick for a bat and old tin cans

Perucho Cepeda was a legend in the Puerto Rican League, winning the 1938–39 batting title with a .465 average. At that time, dark-skinned Latins were excluded from the major leagues. Twenty years later, however, Perucho's son Orlando became a star with the San Francisco Giants.

for baseballs, when a rice salesman named Roberto Marín drove by. Marín was scouting San Antón and other nearby barrios in search of talent for a softball team sponsored by his employer, the Sello Rojo rice company. The first thing he noticed was that one boy "hit those cans pretty far. . . . He never struck out. Bam! Bam! Bam! Tin cans all over the field. . . . I told him to come to [downtown] Carolina to try out for the softball team." The boy was Roberto Clemente. Marín gave him his first uniform, a red-and-white Sello Rojo T-shirt.

In the beginning, Marín's team played Roberto at shortstop because of his strong arm. "He was an outstanding shortstop," according to one observer. "He made sensational plays in the field. His cap would always fall off and the people loved him." Though a fan favorite because of his hustling style and all-out effort in the field, Clemente did not hit much and usually batted eighth in the order. Also, Marín's baseball eye told him that Clemente did not have sufficient fielding range to play shortstop at higher levels of competition and that he would be better off somewhere else on the diamond. But Marín knew that Clemente's hitting would come around in time, as he gained experience and strength.

Clemente moved to the outfield and applied himself with a vengeance to his new position. "I never saw a boy who loved baseball like he did," said Marín. "He spent every hour he could playing. He always carried that ball to squeeze. After games we would stop to drink beer; he always drank milk and then went home to bed." Soon, Clemente became a graceful outfielder and began to develop his unorthodox, opposite-field hitting style. As Marín said, "His name became known for his long hits to right field and for his sensational catches. Everyone had their eyes on him."

Two years after joining the Sello Rojo team, the 16-year-old Clemente caused a sensation with his play at a San Juan softball tournament. Several teams from local amateur baseball leagues became interested in him. Marín recalled, "He was like an un-polished gem. He had a strong arm, speed; he was a complete

Monte Irvin, a star outfielder in the Negro Leagues from 1938 to 1948, also played for the San Juan Senadores during the winter; after Jackie Robinson broke baseball's color line in 1947, Irvin had a standout career with the New York Giants. The young Clemente was called "Monte Irvin" by his friends because of his admiration for the future Hall of Famer.

athlete." Clemente began to play for Juncos in the Puerto Rican Double-A League, a well-known team in a very fast league that was the equal of some mainland professional minor leagues. It was, and still is, extensively scouted by professional teams from both Puerto Rico and the mainland United States.

At the same time that he was playing for Sello Rojo and Juncos, Roberto Clemente also played baseball for Julio Vizcarrondo High School in Carolina. He was a perennial all-star at shortstop. But he attracted more attention at school for his track-and-field heroics. The "Most Valuable Player" on his track team and widely considered a candidate to represent Puerto Rico in the upcoming 1952 Olympic Games in Helsinki, Finland, Clemente triple-jumped a then-outstanding 45 feet and high-jumped 6 feet. As always, his own success seemed to come as a big surprise to Clemente. At an important high school track meet, he had to be talked into entering the 440-yard race against a team from rival Humacao. An old teammate remembered, "He didn't want to, he didn't think he was good enough. We had a good 440 man named Chu-Chu Barbosa, and Humacao's runner was the best on the island. Roberto beat them both. Everybody knew he could do such things; only he didn't know." It would not come as a surprise to any baseball fan who ever saw him make a running catch, stop, whirl 180 degrees, and uncork a throw of uncanny strength and accuracy, that Clemente's best event was the javelin throw. He once made a throw of 195 feet, a remarkable feat for a high school athlete.

Clemente never did get to display his talents in the Olympics because he had other plans. On October 9, 1952, he signed a contract to play professional baseball.

Clemente joined the Santurce Cangrejeros (Crabbers) of the Puerto Rican League in 1952, at the age of 18. Clemente might have signed with a major league team at this time, but major league rules prevented any team from signing him until he finished his final year of high school.

CHAPTER THREE

"Uno Más"

The game that Roberto Clemente loved so much became a career in the fall of 1952, when he was 18 years old and starring for the Juncos team. One day, his old mentor Roberto Marín told him, "*Caramba*, Roberto, I think you're as good or better than many of the pros who play here in the Winter League. I'm going to talk with a friend of mine, Pedrín Zorilla, who owns one of the clubs and is also a scout for the Brooklyn Dodgers."

Zorilla was both more and less than a scout. He owned and ran the Santurce Cangrejeros (Crabbers), who were at the time a winter league powerhouse. Zorilla had founded the team in 1939 with the idea that he would combine Hispanic stars such as Tetelo Vargas with high-quality black players imported from the United States. Ever since the 1880s, the major leagues had refused to hire American blacks—or, for that matter, dark-skinned Hispanics—claiming that they were not good enough to compete. Black players in America were forced to play in their own baseball leagues, called the Negro Leagues. This so-called color line in baseball lasted

Pedrín Zorilla, owner of the Santurce Cangrejeros, poses with the trophies won by his team during the 1951 Caribbean Series. After signing Clemente to a contract, Zorilla carefully limited his playing time. He wanted the youngster to learn the game before he was thrown into pressure situations.

until 1947, when the Brooklyn Dodgers put an end to it by signing Jackie Robinson. Because salaries for black baseball players were very low in the Negro Leagues, owners such as Zorilla could hire them to play winter ball at a bargain price.

Zorilla also made money by developing and exporting local talent from Puerto Rico to the majors, acting as a "bird dog," or free-lance part-time scout, in informal working arrangements with American major league clubs. Originally associated with the New York Giants, Zorilla had sent north such great local players as Orlando Cepeda and Ruben Gomez, both of whom went on to star for the Giants. But now, he was on the side of the Giants' archrivals from across New York City's East River, the Brooklyn Dodgers.

Marín brought the young Clemente to Zorilla's beachfront home in Manatí. The Cangrejeros owner, being a shrewd businessman, shrugged off Marín's enthusiasm over the boy's prospects. After all, if Zorilla did decide to sign him to a contract someday, he didn't want Clemente to have an exaggerated idea of his worth. He did, however, invite him to a joint Cangrejeros–Dodgers tryout being held at Sixto Escobar Stadium a few days later by the chief Latin American scout for the Dodgers, Al Campanis.

Very few of Campanis's baseball prospects had come from open tryouts like the one to which Zorilla invited Clemente in 1952; these are held mostly for public relations value. Every once in a while, a potential major leaguer slips through baseball's immense scouting network and is discovered in an open tryout, but mostly such things happen only in scouts' (and aspiring players') dreams. More typical was the Dodgers' previous tryout in Puerto Rico two years earlier, when not a single player was signed. So Campanis was not prepared for what he saw when Roberto Clemente and 71 other boys and young men lined up in center field for the first of the day's tests—making a long throw to home plate from center field and running the 60-yard dash.

One throw after another sailed lazily toward its target, too high to be cut off by an infielder and too slow to keep major league runners from advancing an extra base. Some throws had good distance but sailed far wide of the plate. Then Clemente stepped up and fired the ball on a straight line into the catcher; Campanis's head turned when he heard the loud *pop!* from the catcher's mitt. "I couldn't believe my eyes," he said later. "This one kid throws a bullet, on the fly." "*Uno más,*" Campanis shouted to Clemente. "One more." Clemente uncorked another perfect throw.

Next was the 60-yard dash, run not in shorts and T-shirts on a hard running track but on grass and in full baseball uniforms. Clemente left the others in the dust and registered a time of 6.4 seconds on Campanis's stopwatch. "Hell, the world's record then was only 6.1. I couldn't believe it," Campanis recalled. "Uno más," he ordered, and again the stopwatch read 6.4.

At this point, the tryout ended for the other players, and only Roberto Clemente was sent up to hit against one of the Dodgers' minor league pitchers. "He hit for 20, 25 minutes," recalled Campanis, who was about to find out how Roberto Marín felt when he first saw the young Clemente crushing tin cans with a stick on a dusty San Antón street: "I'm behind the cage and I'm saying to myself, we gotta sign this guy if he can just hold the bat in his hands. He starts hitting line drives all over the place. I notice the way he's standing in the box, and I figure there's no way he can reach the outside of the plate, so I tell the pitcher to pitch him outside, and the kid swings with both feet off the ground and hits line drives to right and sharp ground balls up the middle."

Campanis considered Clemente the greatest natural athlete he had ever seen. But like Zorilla, he played his cards close to the vest and told Marín that Clemente was a good raw talent who needed polish. Actually, he would have loved to sign Clemente and let the Dodgers' minor league system do the polishing, but there was one problem. Under major league baseball rules, a prospect could not be signed until he graduated from high school, and Clemente had one more year of school to go.

Puerto Rican League teams had no such rule, however. When Pedrín Zorilla went to a Juncos game the following Sunday and saw Clemente line a hit off the outfield fence, make two circus catches in center field, and throw out a runner at home plate, he signed Clemente to a contract with Santurce that would pay him a $400 bonus and $40 per week to learn, as he put it, "how to put his uniform on right." Zorilla wanted Clemente to study the art of professional baseball at the feet of Santurce's veteran players—not, at first, by playing but by watching. In his first season, Clemente came to bat only 77 times, batting .234. There was sound baseball reasoning behind Zorilla's plan, which was designed to shield Clemente's delicate confidence. "I never let the young ones play much," he later explained. "We had great pitchers here. Satchel Paige [one of the greatest of the Negro Leaguers and a future member of the Hall of Fame], pitchers like that. The ball comes to the plate looking like an aspirin tablet. A young boy like Clemente

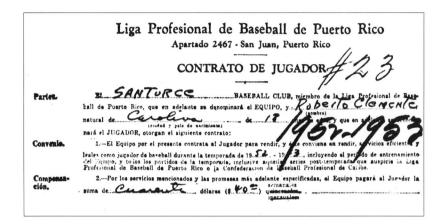

Liga Profesional de Baseball de Puerto Rico

Apartado 2467 · San Juan, Puerto Rico

CONTRATO DE JUGADOR

Clemente's first contract with the Cangrejeros called for a salary of $40 a week. There were other benefits as well: Because owner Pedrín Zorilla also worked as a scout for the Brooklyn Dodgers, he was able to get Clemente a tryout with the big-league club.

strikes out three or four times in a row, he starts asking questions of himself: 'Can I hit? Can I really play?' It is important he does not give himself the wrong answers."

Zorilla and his manager, Buster Clarkson, soon found out that the only question Clemente was asking himself was, Why am I not playing? As the season wore on, he grew tired of sitting on the bench and even threatened to quit the team on several occasions. Clemente's career was saved when Clarkson, whom Clemente always called "Papa," took him under his wing. "The main thing I had to do was keep his spirits up," Clarkson said. "He didn't realize how good he was. But I could see his potential. I had three good outfielders, but I had to give him a chance, and he broke into the regular line-up [later] during the first season I managed in Santurce. . . . I told him he'd be as good as Willie Mays some day. And he was."

Clarkson also helped Clemente polish his baseball technique. "He had a few rough spots," Clarkson remembered, "but he never made the same mistake twice. He had baseball savvy and he listened. He listened to what he was told and he did it." One of Clemente's main "rough spots" as a hitter was a tendency to bail out, or open up the left side of his body too quickly when he swung. To fix this, "Clarkson put a bat behind my left foot to make sure I didn't drag it," Clemente remembered. "He helped me as much as anyone. I was just a kid, but he insisted the older players let me take batting practice." Clarkson's work paid off in a late-season game when, with the bases loaded and the game on the line, he sent Clemente in to pinch-hit against a tough left-handed pitcher. Clemente cleared the bases with a ringing double and spent the remainder of the 1952–53 season in the regular Santurce lineup.

Roberto Clemente started the 1953–54 season as the Cangrejeros' regular right fielder, but he was still fuming at his employer over what he considered a slight. When the Cangrejeros traveled to Havana, Cuba, to represent Puerto Rico in the Caribbean Series, Zorilla had left behind Clemente and some of Santurce's other young players and replaced them with veterans from other teams. (Apparently he chose well, because Santurce won the series for Puerto Rico.) As he would so many times in the future, Clemente turned his anger against his opponents on the baseball diamond. Barely 19 years old and playing everyday against near–major league competition, Clemente batted .288, with 17 extra-base hits and 27 RBIs in 219 at-bats.

Before the season was over, the word on Roberto Clemente was out, and men from the major leagues began knocking at his door. In the end, it came down to a bidding war between the Giants and Dodgers. Clemente settled the issue by announcing that he would accept the Dodgers' $10,000 bonus and $5,000 per year salary, a deal that was very generous for the time. A few days later, Milwaukee Braves scout Luis Rodríguez-Olmo shocked Clemente with an offer of $28,000. Clemente was torn between his handshake commitment to the Dodgers and what seemed like an unthinkably large amount of money. He asked his mother for advice, and she replied, "If you gave your word to one team, then you must keep your word." That was that. Besides, Clemente reflected, "Brooklyn was a famous team. I wanted to play for the Dodgers. I did not know much about Milwaukee then. I did not even know where Milwaukee was."

There were other things Clemente did not know. One of them was that the Dodgers' primary interest was not so much in playing him (they had an outfield of Carl Furillo, the National League batting champion; Duke Snider, who had hit 42 home runs in 1953; and Cuban-born Sandy Amoros, a hot prospect) as in keeping him out of the hands of the rival Giants. As Dodgers vice-president Buzzy Bavasi later admitted, "We didn't want the Giants to have Clemente and Willie Mays in the same outfield. It was a cheap deal for us." Thus, on February 19, 1954, Pedrín Zorilla formalized Clemente's Brooklyn contract in the form of a telegram to the United States which was cosigned by the underage Clemente and his proud father, who indicated his consent with an *X*. Now legally the property of the Brooklyn Dodgers, Clemente was assigned for the upcoming 1954 season to the Dodgers' top minor league club, the Montreal Royals—the same team Jackie Robinson had played for in 1946 when he integrated the International League. A year later, Clemente would be in the major leagues.

For a young American player, and for the average Puerto Rican player today, this is where the story of a winter league career ends. The Puerto Rican League no longer contains top-notch, veteran teams that uphold the honor of communities such as San Juan, Caguas, and Santurce in stadiums packed with rabid fans who, as Pedrín Zorilla once said, "if they would have to kill someone for their team, would do it gladly." More and more like the mainland minor leagues, the Puerto Rican League serves as a school for prospects or as a proving ground for young players trying to impress a major league club or learn a new position. And when today's Puerto Rican players make it to the major leagues, they often earn large salaries very quickly and no longer feel the same obligation to perform for their friends and compatriots. As a result, the sophisticated Puerto Rican baseball fans prefer to stay home and watch major league baseball on television, rather than pay to see what they consider to be an inferior product.

But for Roberto Clemente and contemporaries such as Orlando Cepeda or Vic Power, things were very different. After nearly every major league season, no matter how tired he was, Clemente managed to return to Puerto Rico to play the season—or, if he was injured, to appear in at least a few games. Playing for Santurce and Caguas, he batted .396 and won the league batting title in 1956–57. With San Juan from the 1960–61 season through 1970–71, Clemente hit well over .300 and served a stint as manager.

Many outstanding major leaguers played in Puerto Rico during the winter. The 1954–55 Santurce Cangrejeros included (left to right) Willie Mays, Clemente, Buster Clarkson (manager), Bob Thurman, and George Crowe. Clemente later asserted that this team was as good as the 1971 world champion Pittsburgh Pirates.

Unquestionably the high point of Clemente's Puerto Rican League career, however, was playing right field for the 1954–55 Santurce Cangrejeros. This was a team that many consider the finest winter league team ever—and possibly the finest team that has ever played anywhere outside the major leagues. In addition to Clemente, the team featured major leaguers such as Willie Mays, Willie Kirkland, Don Zimmer, George Crowe, Bob Thurman, Toothpick Sam Jones, and Ruben Gomez. After rolling over the local competition, this team went to Venezuela and won Puerto Rico's third consecutive Caribbean Series. Many years later, when asked if he had ever seen a lineup as powerful as that of the 1971 Pittsburgh Pirates, Clemente replied, "Yes, the 1954–55 Santurce Crabbers."

"Every Puerto Rican is a Roberto Clemente fan," stated the *Sporting News* in a 1966 article, referring to the stir on the island caused by the hot National League batting race between Clemente and the Dominican Matty Alou. Each of Clemente's major league achievements and honors was relished back home. Most of all, the opportunity for Puerto Ricans to watch him play in person during the winter made for an especially close bond between them and Clemente. New Yorker Felix "Gene" DeJesus, a former amateur ballplayer who grew up in San Juan rooting for Clemente and the San Juan Senadores, remembered the first time he saw the effect of his hero's presence on the fans: "It was a Sunday doubleheader against [archrival] Santurce and I got there early to watch batting practice. You enter Hiram Bithorn Stadium at field level and, as I walked in, I remember thinking, 'Where is everybody?' because I knew there would be a big crowd but I didn't hear anything. What I saw when I got inside was electrifying. The whole stadium was silent, as though they were watching a ballet. Everyone was watching Roberto Clemente, alone as if in the middle of a stage, hitting line drives all over the field. I will never forget the feeling of that afternoon and the 'pow-pow-pow' sound of the baseballs coming off his bat."

When Clemente scored the winning run for Santurce in the 1954 championship game, he had already signed a contract with the Brooklyn Dodgers. Shortly afterward, the 20-year-old star boarded a plane for Montreal, Canada, where he joined the Dodgers' top minor league club, the Royals.

CHAPTER FOUR

"Bobby Clemente"

On a spring day in 1954, the 19-year-old Roberto Clemente left his family and friends to try to make his way in the unfamiliar, English-speaking world of American baseball, 2,000 miles to the north. To make things more difficult, he was not going to New York, where hundreds of thousands of fans spoke his language. Clemente was headed for Montreal. A sophisticated, historic city on the Saint Lawrence River, Montreal is the cultural heart of Quebec, Canada's French-speaking province. Thus, Montreal presented Clemente with a double language barrier—one at the ballpark and another away from it. He knew a few words of English, mostly baseball terms, but when he changed out of his blue-and-white Montreal Royals uniform into street clothes, even those few words were often useless. The smallest tasks of everyday life—from reading menus to riding buses to doing his laundry—became a big challenge.

Still, Clemente was a professional baseball player, and the ballpark should have been an oasis for him. Unfortunately, almost as soon as he arrived, things became even more confusing there.

In the opinion of the Royals manager, Max Macon, Clemente was "a wild-swinging kid, but he just radiated ability." What puzzled Clemente was Macon's apparent refusal to let him show that ability on the field. Just as he had in his first season with Santurce, Clemente rode the bench. And he was not sitting down because the Royals had an all-star outfield; no one was likely to mistake Montreal's Gino Cimoli and Dick Whitman for Willie Mays and Bob Thurman.

One night early in the season, Clemente thought he was going to get his big chance: He was coming to bat in the first inning with the bases loaded. "They called time," Clemente later remembered, "and called for a pinch hitter." On another occasion, Macon left him in for an entire game, and Clemente slammed three triples. But his name was not on the lineup card the next night, or the night after that. The last straw for Clemente came when Macon hit upon the novel strategy of playing the young outfielder from Puerto Rico only when the weather was cool. In Richmond, Virginia, where the heat was to his liking, he sat. However, if the Royals were playing in upstate New York against Syracuse, a team loaded with tough, right-handed pitching, Clemente was guaranteed to play.

Finally, Clemente called Roberto Marín and announced that he was going to quit. Thinking that this was another case of Clemente rebelling against the better judgment of superiors who, like Pedrín Zorilla, had his best interests at heart, Marín told him, "Take it easy, you're just a kid." Clemente stayed in Montreal, and Macon left him on the bench for nearly all of the last 25 games in the Royals' schedule. Not surprisingly, the disillusioned Clemente finished the year with a poor record. For the year, his numbers show a .257 batting average with 12 RBIs and 10 extra-base hits in 87 games; he recorded only 148 official at-bats.

Eventually, Clemente figured out what was happening: "The idea was to make me look bad. . . . They wanted to make me mad enough to go home." This may sound far-fetched, but it was probably true. Clemente did not know it, but during the 1954

Clemente's unhappy expression in this photograph sums up his year with the Montreal Royals. Alone in a strange city where few people spoke Spanish, he was given little playing time by the Royals manager. After the season, the Pittsburgh Pirates drafted Clemente and promised him a chance to prove himself.

season he was the subject of behind-the-scenes maneuvering that belonged to the hard-boiled business side of American baseball.

From the moment Clemente had signed his contract, he had become not just Roberto Clemente, human being, or Roberto Clemente, ballplayer, but—in the phrase of the wire-service report that announced his contract with the Dodgers—Roberto Clemente, "negro bonus player from Puerto Rico." The color of his skin was important because, in spite of Jackie Robinson, major league teams in 1954 were still very fearful about the issue of race. There were rumors that Brooklyn, the team with the most black players, was operating under an unspoken racial quota guaranteeing that black players would never be a majority on the field. This explained why it seemed to many fans that whenever the team pitched Don Newcombe, who was black, either Roy Campanella, Junior Gilliam, or another of the Dodgers' four black position players would be out of the lineup with a mysterious minor injury. After all, this was the mid-1950s. The U.S. Supreme Court did not ban segregation in public schools until 1954; the major leagues appointed their first black umpire only in 1965 and their first black manager in 1974. Bill White, the majors' first black league president, took office in 1989.

Clemente's $10,000 bonus was another important factor in the story. According to the baseball rules of the time, any team that signed a player for a bonus larger than $4,000 had to keep him with the major league team for his entire rookie season. If they sent him to the minors, they would risk losing him in a special draft at the end of the year. All major league teams drafted in reverse order of their place in the standings—in other words, the worst team got first pick—and could acquire any available bonus player in this category for a price of $4,000.

Looking back on all this later, Clemente still wondered how the Dodgers could have thought they could hide him in Montreal; after all, no matter how bad his numbers might be, 7 or 8 teams had offered him much more than $4,000 to sign with them only a year before. "Everybody knew what I could do," Clemente later remarked. "The Dodgers knew they were going to lose me in the draft. . . . As soon as they put me on the Montreal roster, they knew one of those teams was going to get me."

Perhaps the Dodgers figured that Clemente might get so frustrated that he would walk out on the Royals and go home; this would mean that he would remain Dodgers property and would no longer be subject to the draft. Another possibility was that some team might draft one of Montreal's other talented players, such as pitcher Joe Black. That would place Clemente off-limits because a team could lose only one player from each of its minor league teams. Finally, if none of these things happened, at least Clemente would never play for the rival New York Giants. Because the Giants were a contending team in 1954 (indeed, they went on to beat out Brooklyn for the pennant), they would pick late in the draft, long after Clemente was gone. As Dodgers executive Buzzy Bavasi later explained, "So all right, it cost us $6,000, but the Giants didn't get him, which was the important thing."

As it turned out, the perennial last place finishers, the Pittsburgh Pirates, were watching Roberto Clemente as carefully as they could, considering that he was being played so infrequently by Max Macon. The Pirates' first report on Clemente came from scout Clyde Sukeforth, who had been sent to look at Joe Black. Unfortunately for the Dodgers, Sukeforth saw Clemente practicing throws from the outfield before the game. "I couldn't take my eyes off him," said Sukeforth. "Later in the game he was used as a pinch hitter and I liked his swing. He impressed me a great deal. I started asking questions and learned he was a bonus player and would be available for the draft."

Clemente knew nothing of this until the last day of the season, when another Pirates scout, Howie Haak, arrived to watch the Royals in order to double-check on Sukeforth's glowing recommendation. Macon knew why Haak was there and made sure that he never got more than a fleeting glimpse of Clemente. Clemente was in the starting lineup that day, batting seventh, but as he got ready to hit with two men on base in the middle of a big first inning rally, once again Macon called him back and replaced him with a pinch hitter. When Haak went to the team hotel after the game, he found an indignant Clemente packing his bags for Puerto Rico. He was ready to walk out on the Royals before the start of the International League playoffs. "Roberto," Haak argued in his broken Spanish, "if you go home now, you will be placed on the ineligible list. Then no one will be able to pick you in the draft. Finish the season, then go home, and you will be playing in Pittsburgh next year, playing everyday for the Pirates."

Clemente listened to Haak and unpacked his bags. As promised, on November 22, 1954, the Pittsburgh Pirates used their first pick in the draft to purchase Roberto Clemente from Brooklyn for $4,000. As Clemente confessed later, "I didn't even know where Pittsburgh was."

Any baseball fan could have told Clemente where Pittsburgh was—in the basement of the National League, as usual. Almost completely devoid of talent at both the major league and minor

The flamboyant Branch Rickey (center) was hired in 1951 to rebuild the lowly Pirates. Rickey infuriated Pittsburgh fans by trading popular slugger Ralph Kiner (right), but he acquired a group of young players who later made the Pirates into champions—chief among them Roberto Clemente.

league levels, the Pittsburgh Pirates had reached a crisis in 1950, when they finished last with 57 wins and 96 losses. In desperation they turned to Branch Rickey, the guru of modern baseball organization and the architect of two of the 20th century's greatest dynasties, the Dodgers and the Cardinals. He was also the man who had signed Jackie Robinson to a major league contract. Pittsburgh hired him away from Brooklyn before the start of the 1951 season and named him general manager, with broad powers over every aspect of the team.

In the short term, there was little improvement; the Pirates finished last in 1952, 1953, 1954, and 1955. Ticket sales plummeted after Rickey outraged the fans in 1953 by trading away Ralph Kiner, one of the most popular players in Pirates history and their greatest all-time home run hitter. Most of the Pirates veterans hated Rickey for being a cheapskate when it came to their salaries. He once told Kiner, when the slugger asked for a raise: "We finished last with you; we can finish last without you." After the 1955 season, the Pirates finally ran out of patience and fired Rickey.

Despite his failure to improve the standing of the team, Rickey had rebuilt the Pirates' minor league system. The 1955 team already contained the ingredients for the Pirates' rebirth—shortstop Dick Groat, outfielder Frank Thomas, and pitchers Bob Friend, Vern Law, and Elroy Face, not one of them past his mid-twenties. Second baseman Bill Mazeroski was in the minors. These players formed the nucleus that lifted the team to second place in 1958 and then to the National League pennant in 1960. Branch Rickey left one more legacy, a player who bridged the gap between the championship seasons of 1960 and 1971 and who almost made the city of Pittsburgh forgive Rickey for trading Kiner—Roberto Clemente.

When Clemente joined the Pirates in 1955, they had lost more than 100 games for 3 years in a row. As the season opened, manager Fred Haney quickly concluded that the 1955 team was unlikely to do any better. Before long, he started benching the veterans in order to see what the youngsters could do. Just 3 days into the

Clemente is tagged out while trying to score against the Chicago Cubs in June 1955. During Clemente's rookie season, the Pirates stumbled to their fourth straight last-place finish. Despite hitting a modest .255 for the year, Clemente played 124 games and learned the fine points of major league baseball.

season—with the Pirates sporting a record of 0 and 3—Clemente broke into the starting outfield against the Dodgers, replacing Roman Mejias in right. In front of 20,499 fans at stately old Forbes Field in Pittsburgh, Clemente hit a ball into the hole on the left side of the infield and beat Pee Wee Reese's throw to first, chalking up his first base hit. Over the years, Clemente would do far worse damage to the Dodgers; he always seemed to play extra hard against his former team, as if determined to make them regret the way they had treated him in 1954.

Clemente carried with him from his days in Montreal a fierce, raging desire to succeed. "He was only 20, and he was sensitive to the general conditions," recalled former Pittsburgh executive Joe L. Brown. "He was stimulated by challenge, and we weren't competitive." Eight games into the 1955 campaign, the pitiful Pirates were 0 and 8; Clemente, though batting .360, was consumed by anger and disappointment. He began to take his feelings out on the team's plastic batting helmets. He crushed them, heaved them, and kicked them. He shattered them with his bat. After Clemente had destroyed 22 helmets, Haney warned him, "I don't mind you tearing up your own clothes if you want to, but if you're going to destroy club property, you're going to pay for it." Informed that he would be fined $10 per broken helmet, Clemente learned to control himself. "I do not make so much money," he said. "I'll stop breaking the hats."

Next in Clemente's line of fire were the umpires. The worst incident came in Philadelphia, when he was called out on strikes by umpire Bill Jackowski on an outside pitch. Clemente complained, and Jackowski argued back; soon, Clemente was going after Jackowski while the Pirates' third base coach tried to hold him back. Clemente managed to land one blow, for which he was fined $250 and suspended 5 days by National League president Warren Giles. On numerous other occasions throughout the early years of his career, Clemente boiled over and was ejected from the game.

Clemente finished his first season in the major leagues with a fairly unimpressive .255 batting average, 23 doubles, and 5 home runs in 124 games. But he was young—he turned 21 that August—and still learning. The first lesson was to tailor his hitting style to his spacious home park. As Clemente recalled, "When I first saw Forbes Field, I said, 'Forget home runs.' I was strong, but nobody is that strong. I became a line-drive hitter." Throughout the first five years of his career, Clemente's number one weakness as a hitter was typical of young players—bad strike zone judgment. He whiffed 60 times in 1955 and 58 times in 1956 while drawing a total of only 31 walks. In the field, though, Clemente's right arm wasted no time in introducing itself to base runners around the league; he recorded 10 assists in his first 50 games. And he quickly mastered the art of playing balls off Forbes Field's right-field wall, whose peculiar contours produced a bewildering variety of caroms. He took endless outfield practice. "I knew if I could not play right field well, I might not play regularly. I didn't like that much."

A fierce competitor, Clemente did not take losing lightly in his early days with the Pirates: He argued with umpires and smashed batting helmets with regularity. Finally, when manager Fred Haney threatened to charge him $10 for each helmet he broke, Clemente decided to control his temper.

Clemente became the Pirates' regular right fielder for good after 1955. But from then until 1960, his career followed a frustrating up-and-down pattern. One reason was that Clemente was battling against an enemy more intransigent than umpires or league officials—his own health.

After playing in 147 games in 1956 and raising his average to .311, Clemente slipped to .253 in 1957. He was limited to only 111 games by a disk condition in his lower back that dated to a car accident before the 1954 season. His back problems, which sidelined Clemente many times throughout his long career, caused him so much pain during the 1956–57 off-season that he thought seriously of quitting baseball and returning to school. "Finally," Clemente remembered, "I told my mother and father, 'I will try it for one more year. If I still hurt, then I quit.'" In 1958, Clemente rebounded to play 140 games, bat .289, and collect 40 extra-base hits; he scored a career-high 69 runs and drove in 50 to help Pittsburgh to 84 wins and second place in the standings, its highest finish since World War II. Clemente also recorded 22 assists to lead the National League in that category for the first of 5 times. But Clemente and the Pirates took a step backward in 1959, when he was limited to 105 games by surgery to remove bone chips that had been floating in his elbow since his javelin-throwing days. The team slipped to fourth place.

Another factor in Clemente's slow development was his inability to adjust to life off the field. Pittsburgh, a blue-collar town with almost no Hispanics and a small black community that in the 1950s was mostly confined to a neighborhood called the Hill, was no more hospitable than Montreal had been. Aside from the usual problems with food, apartments, and transportation, Clemente was often lonely and confused by the coldness and the racial and ethnic prejudice that he encountered in America. Once, on a trip to New York City, Clemente went shopping for some furniture. A salesman quickly ushered him aside and showed him some models that were much cheaper than the ones he had been looking at. When Clemente asked why, the salesman told him, "Well, you don't have enough money to buy that." After he took $5,000 out of his wallet and someone told the salesman who Clemente was, the salesman apologized and explained that he had thought that Clemente was "just another Puerto Rican." Clemente walked out of the store.

Ironically, this happened on the same day that the Mets staged a Roberto Clemente Night at Shea Stadium and sold 44,000 tickets, mostly to Puerto Ricans living in New York. As Clemente told a reporter, "We [Hispanic players] need time to get adjusted here like you would need time to get adjusted in our countries. We lead different lives in the United States. We're always meeting new people, seeing new faces. Everything is strange. The language barrier is great at first and we have trouble ordering food in restaurants. In the early days, segregation baffled us, but this has eased much in recent years. You have no idea how this held some of us back, however. We Latins are people of high emotions and coming to this country we need time to settle down emotionally. Once we're relaxed and have no problems, we can play baseball well. The people who never run into these problems don't have any idea at all what kind of an ordeal this can be."

By 1960, Roberto Clemente was beginning to play baseball very well indeed, and as unlikely as it might have seemed at the time, the Pirates were about to ride his talent to dizzying heights. Branch Rickey's orphans grew up to have the best hitting and the best pitching in the National League, winning 95 games and the pennant. Most remarkably, they went on to defeat the seemingly unbeatable New York Yankees on Bill Mazeroski's home run over the left-field wall at Forbes Field, in the bottom of the ninth inning of the seventh game of the World Series.

The heart of the 1960 Pirates was the trio of shortstop Dick Groat, who won the batting title at .325; third baseman Don Hoak, who hit 16 home runs and led the team in runs scored with 97; and

Bill Mazeroski sprints into the arms of teammates and fans after winning the 1960 World Series with a dramatic home run in the bottom of the ninth inning. Clemente batted .310 for the series as the Pirates upset the mighty New York Yankees in 7 games.

Roberto Clemente. For Clemente, 1960 was the first season in which he began to truly deliver on his great promise. He batted .314, with 16 homers, 89 runs scored, and a team-high 94 RBIs. Many of those RBIs came in the biggest games of the year. Clemente's home run on July 25 helped beat the surging St. Louis Cardinals. Late in the season, he hit a cluster of three home runs to pull the team out of a tailspin and stop a four-game losing streak on the West Coast. At one point, Clemente spent five days in the hospital after making a game-saving catch off Willie Mays while smashing face-first into a concrete wall; Pittsburgh's lead shrunk from seven games to two. Still, he gave little of the credit to himself, saying, "To win, you must play as a family. We played as a family."

Unfortunately, not everybody felt the same way. There were rumors that Dick Groat, who had missed a month of the pennant race with an injury, was campaigning behind the scenes for the Most Valuable Player Award, which is determined by a vote of the nation's sportswriters and which frequently goes to the best player on the pennant-winning team. At the same time, one of the Pittsburgh writers circulated letters arguing against Clemente as a potential MVP. At the time, many of the writers in Pittsburgh and elsewhere were uncomfortable with the influx of blacks and Hispanics into major league baseball—as exemplified by their unwillingness to use Clemente's actual first name in their stories. For years, he was "Bob Clemente" or "Bobby Clemente" in print.

Roberto Clemente was a particular problem because he spoke out when he felt he was being slighted. According to Roy McHugh, former sports editor of the *Pittsburgh Press,* "I always had to stand there and listen to his five-minute denunciation of sportswriters. I got tired of it. . . . It got so tiresome, I avoided him unless I had to talk to him." It became easier to ignore Clemente than to hear

Shortstop Dick Groat goes high in the air while turning a double play. Groat won the 1960 Most Valuable Player Award, with Pirates third baseman Don Hoak finishing second in the voting. Clemente had expected this to happen, but he was outraged when he himself did no better than eighth place.

what he had to say. As a result, he became almost invisible in the sports pages. A reader can go through back issues of the *Sporting News* from the late 1950s to the early 1960s and find countless articles on Groat, Hoak, Law, and Mazeroski but hardly run across any mention of Clemente. This was true no matter what he did on the field. In the thrilling 1961 All-Star Game at San Francisco's Candlestick Park, Clemente hit a triple and drove in two runs, including the winning run in the bottom of the 10th inning. But in most newspaper accounts, the big event of the day was a gust of wind that blew pitcher Stu Miller off the mound in the top of the ninth inning.

As he rested at home in Puerto Rico in the weeks following the 1960 World Series, Clemente may not have expected to win the MVP vote against two popular white players such as Groat and Hoak. In fact, a reasonable argument could have been made for any one of the three Pirates. But when the vote was announced, Clemente found the result hard to believe. The winner was Dick Groat, with Hoak in second place. Then came the Giants' Willie Mays and the Cubs' Ernie Banks. Inexplicably, Clemente finished eighth, trailing Cardinals Lindy McDaniel and Ken Boyer and fellow Pirate Vern Law. In public, Clemente was composed: "I didn't receive the recognition I felt was due me," he said. "It is not a matter of false vanity or anything of the kind. I felt I had a very good year and I also felt that it was overlooked." But on the inside, he was deeply insulted. "I believe that's what hurt Roberto," said Danny Murtaugh, the Pirates manager at the time. "He thought he should have been MVP. He changed after that." The following spring, all of the other Pirates were sporting their new, jewel-studded World Series rings. No one ever saw Clemente wear his.

Clemente poses with Cuban-born pitcher Gonzalo "Cholly" Naranjo before a game with the New York Giants in 1956. From the beginning of his major league career, Clemente championed the cause of Latin ballplayers and freely criticized teammates, opponents, and sportswriters for acts of discrimination.

CHAPTER FIVE

Clemente Versus Baseball

The 1960 MVP vote was a strong blow to Clemente's pride. But it was only one episode in a long-running battle that Clemente fought with reporters, umpires, and even members of his own team over his 18 years in the major leagues. There were periods when it seemed to Clemente that his life in the mainland United States was a constant uphill battle against a culture that refused to accept the idea that one of the heroes of its national game could be black, or Hispanic, or both. Like most successful athletes, Roberto Clemente was a driven person. He was very sensitive to any personal criticism, slight, or withholding of recognition. And he responded to off-the-field attacks in the same way that he responded to a brushback pitch—by counterattacking so fiercely that his opponent would regret ever having taken him on.

Clemente began his career fighting against Pittsburgh team-mates who teased and ridiculed him unmercifully. This was part of the usual way that rookies are treated in the major leagues, a verbal baptism of fire that has been traditional in baseball for more than a century. It serves two main purposes: First, it is a kind of initiation ritual that reinforces the psychological unity of the team; and second, it is a relatively harmless way for players to express feelings of hostility toward other players they dislike or who may be a threat to take away their job. At times, though, it can become very rough. Friends of the great Ty Cobb believed that the anger and bitterness he showed throughout his career had a lot to do with the razzing he suffered at the hands of Detroit Tigers teammates in 1905, when Cobb was a rookie. Perhaps in part because of the language barrier that separated him from most of his teammates, Clemente could not understand what was happening to him: "Why?" he asked a friend about all the insults he had to endure. "I never hurt anyone in my life."

Clemente's frequent injuries and missed playing time gave his teammates ammunition for their attacks. As he later remembered, "Sometimes I got mad at people, [like] when I was hurt and everyone called me Jake [a ballplayers' expression for a player who fakes injury]. I didn't like that. I wanted to play but my back hurt lots of times and I couldn't play. You can still feel the bone chips in my elbow. That's why I throw the ball underhand sometimes. That way it doesn't hurt my arm."

Ironically, Clemente hurt his own cause by playing so well when he was in the lineup. It was always a point of pride to Clemente that if he was well enough to put on a uniform, no matter how much he hurt, he always produced. No one ever accused him—even once— of loafing or going half-speed on the field. His 1955 teammates, however, took this as meaning that Clemente was selfish and would only play if he was 100 percent healthy.

Clemente was convinced that some of his teammates' attitudes toward him had to do with race. Not that they called him any names to his face, but during games Clemente suffered when some of the white Pittsburgh players hurled vicious racial insults at black opponents. According to Clemente, there were times when he and Roman Mejias, who was Cuban, challenged the rest of the team

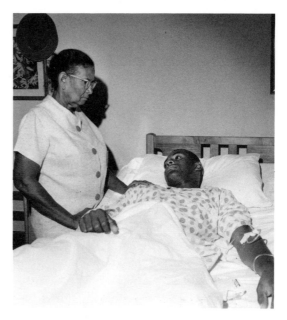

Luisa Clemente visits her son in a Puerto Rican hospital in March 1965. A case of malaria caused Clemente to miss spring training, but he came back that year to win his second batting title in a row. Clemente deeply resented any suggestion that he shied away from playing when he was ill or injured.

right in the dugout. "A lot of the players didn't like us because we were not white," he said. "They made remarks about the colored fellows on the other teams." For the first time, Clemente learned the full meaning of the word *nigger*. "Sometimes I acted like I didn't hear it," Clemente said. "But I heard it. I heard it."

Clemente also battled through rocky relationships with many of the seven men who managed the Pirates during his career, starting with Fred Haney. Danny Murtaugh had the longest tenure at the helm, managing the Pirates from 1956 until 1964. For most of that time, he seemed to be skeptical that Clemente was telling the truth whenever he complained of an injury. One day in 1963, for example, Clemente told a reporter that he was feeling run down from the lingering effects of a case of food poisoning. Even though he had never asked out of the Pirates lineup, Clemente found himself called into the manager's office to face an angry Murtaugh, who told him to take a few days off. "You let me know when you're ready to play again," Murtaugh said in a sarcastic tone. "You're making too much money to sit on the bench. The next time you feel like playing you'll play and you'll play every day until I say you won't play."

"You talk like I don't want to play baseball," answered a bewildered Clemente.

"I don't care what you think, and that's all I'm going to say," the manager replied.

Another time, Clemente removed himself from a game when he discovered that he could not run on a badly cut ankle that had recently been stitched up. Murtaugh fined him $650. "Nobody had better years under Murtaugh than me," Clemente later said. "But he acted like he didn't appreciate me. . . . Murtaugh had no respect for me and I had no respect for him."

In the beginning, Clemente's relationship with Harry Walker, who succeeded Murtaugh in 1965, was no better. The main problem was that Walker had come into the job influenced, as he

Danny Murtaugh managed the Pirates from 1956 through 1964 and often feuded with Clemente. However, when Murtaugh came back for another term as manager in 1970, the two men developed a mutual respect. "When you've got a .340 hitter, you learn to get along with him," Murtaugh remarked.

admitted later, by "rumors that Clemente was hard to get along with." And Clemente got off to a very bad start in 1965 because of malaria, which he had contracted during a trip to the Dominican Republic the previous winter. Eventually, however, both Murtaugh and Walker came to better understand their number one player. After an angry meeting in Chicago in 1965 in which Clemente and Walker cleared the air, Walker remembered, "From that point on, we communicated with each other and believed in each other. I've never lied to him. I always tried to be fair and I think that means a lot to someone as high-spirited as Clemente." Clemente went on to win the 1965 National League batting title.

When Murtaugh came out of retirement to manage the Pirates again in 1970, he and Clemente not only made up but became good friends. "When you've got a .340 hitter," Murtaugh said, "you learn to get along with him." According to Clemente, what really changed Murtaugh was the manager's coming down with back trouble himself. "He was undergoing treatment for his back," Clemente recalled, "and he said to me, 'Now I understand what you've been going through for the past five years.' Finally, Murtaugh understood how I had felt when he criticized me. A hypochondriac [one who suffers from imaginary ailments] does not produce, and I produced." As Murtaugh later explained, "There was a language barrier at the start. Ignorance on both sides. But time took care of that. He was such a truthful man, it backfired on him sometimes. If you asked him if his shoulder hurt, he'd say 'Yes, it does.' Then he'd go out and throw a guy out at the plate. That's how he got the hypochondriac label."

As he grew older and became an established big-league star —and learned to speak much better English—Clemente made peace with his teammates as well. As Groat, Hoak, and the other members of the teams of 1958 and 1960 gradually retired or were traded, a new generation of Pirates came along. The younger players looked up to Clemente as a team leader, and he accepted the responsibility of setting an example for them. As outfielder

Clemente seems at ease in this session with reporters, but his relations with the press were often stormy. Some sportswriters had difficulty accepting the influx of black and Latin players into the major leagues; Clemente was furious when one writer referred to him in print as a "Puerto Rican hot dog."

Gene Clines put it after the 1971 World Series: "You watch Roberto and you can't help getting all psyched. There's the old man out there busting his ass on every play of the game. Look, I'm 25. If he can play like that, shouldn't I?"

But with some members of the press and the radio and television media, Clemente was never able to make friends. Long after he proved himself to his fellow players and to his managers, reporters covering the Pirates refused to let go of the idea that Clemente was a hypochondriac and, in the ugly phrase that one writer used in a spring training story, a "Puerto Rican hot dog." *Hot dog* is a scornful term for a player who shows off on the field or does things differently, such as catching a fly ball with one hand or down at the waist. The idea goes back to the pre–Jackie Robinson days, when the values of white, American-born players were baseball's values. Clemente came from a culture where things were done a little differently, and as Joe L. Brown said of the conservative 1950s, "Anyone who was different was automatically wrong." Today, baseball has come to terms with its show business aspects, and there is greater tolerance for individual differences in style; the only standard is, in the words of former manager Dick Williams, "If you're going to hot dog, fine. . . . But you better make the catch." Clemente always made the catch.

Although he was largely ignored by the press during his early years, by the 1960s Clemente was too important a player not to be covered. Unfortunately, he did not usually like the kind of attention he got. One day, he blew up at a question from a reporter named Dick Stockton, who had referred obliquely to Clemente's supposed hypochondria and suggested that he was not a "team player." "You say maybe I'm not a team player," Clemente heatedly replied. "I won four batting titles. I kill myself in the outfield. . . . I play when I'm hurt. What more do you want from me? Did any ballplayer come up to you and say that I am not a team player? Who said that? The writers, right? . . . You know why? Because they are trying to create a bad image for me. You know what they have against me? Because I am black and Puerto Rican. I am proud to be Puerto Rican."

Clemente was so frustrated because no matter how he dealt with the press, he could not win. If he cooperated, said teammate Bill Mazeroski, "they tried to make him look like an ass by getting him to say controversial things and then they wrote how the 'Puerto Rican hot dog' was popping off again. He was just learning to handle the language, and writers who couldn't speak three words of Spanish tried to make him look silly."

When quoting Clemente, the Pittsburgh writers outdid themselves. One writer came up with the following version of how Clemente talked: "I no play so gut yet. Me like hot weather, veree hot. I no run fast cold weather. No get warm in cold. No get warm, no play gut. You see." This naturally infuriated Clemente, who said,

"I never talk like that; they just want to sell newspapers. Anytime a fellow comes from Puerto Rico, they want to create an image. They say 'Hey, he talks funny.' But if they go to Puerto Rico, they don't talk like us. I don't have a master's degree, but I'm not a dumbhead." To some reporters who indulged in this kind of amateur phonetics, Clemente would suggest that they interview him in Spanish and see how intelligent they sounded.

According to baseball historian Robert Smith: "Latin boys had never been taught to cultivate the 'Gee, fellows, I was pretty lucky' brand of manly self deprecation. . . . So when old-time writers and commentators asked a Latin hero how he rated himself against the great men who had gone before, they were often abashed and outraged to hear that the young outlander thought he was just as good or maybe better. . . . In the late 1960s . . . Roberto Clemente of Pittsburgh was certainly as good a baseball player as any living fan had ever set his eyes on. . . . He lost points in the books of some of his examiners, however, when he unashamedly professed that fact. . . . He simply allowed that no one he knew of in the game could hit, run, throw or play the outfield any better than he could. This simple fact stood uncontroverted, yet there were people who resented Clemente's pointing it out. The real oddity, however, was that so few others had made note of it."

Through all of his battles, there was one group that Roberto Clemente never fought or had trouble communicating with—the Pittsburgh fans. The fans never worried too much about whether Clemente was a good interviewee, or what sportswriters thought of him, or even whether he was third or eighth in the MVP balloting; they only cared about how hard and how splendidly he played for them. Clemente had always felt close to the fans, going back to his friendless rookie year, when he would spend hours and hours signing autographs because, he said, "I had nothing else to do." Once, after a game, he took an unemployed factory worker, a complete stranger, out to dinner; another time, he gave a lift home to a fan in a wheelchair.

Clemente is mobbed by autograph seekers at Pittsburgh's Forbes Field in 1962. Despite his battles with managers, teammates, and reporters, Clemente never had a problem with the fans. They appreciated his all-out style of play, and he never forgot that they spent their hard-earned money to watch him.

After the seventh game of the 1960 World Series, Clemente changed quickly into street clothes and left his victorious teammates, who were enjoying the traditional champagne-spraying locker-room celebration. Many of them grumbled about this, and some reporters wrote that he had shown disrespect to his teammates by rushing off to Puerto Rico. This was not true. As he was fond of doing back home, Clemente had gone into the streets to join the fans, who in this case were putting on a raucous, horn-blowing, confetti-throwing party to celebrate the end of 35 years of losing baseball. The happy throngs brought the city of Pittsburgh to a complete halt. "I came out of the clubhouse," Clemente later recalled, "and saw all those thousands of fans in the streets. It was something you cannot describe. I did not feel like a player at the time. I felt like one of those persons, and I walked the streets among them."

The National League outfield in the 1961 All-Star Game in San Franciso consisted of Clemente, Willie Mays (center), and Henry Aaron. This was Clemente's first appearance as an all-star, and he made the most of it, hitting a triple, a sacrifice fly, and a 10th-inning game-winning single.

CHAPTER SIX

Most Valuable Player

The world champion Pittsburgh Pirates entered the 1961 season confident that they could be one of the rare exceptions to one of baseball's oldest adages: "It's hard to repeat." After a championship season, the following year often brings a falling-off in intensity and performance. One cause of this is the physical and mental exhaustion left over from the strain of a pennant race and the pressures of postseason play. Another cause is simple human nature; it is much harder to motivate players who have had their fill of success than players who are still hungry.

As for the Pirates of 1961, their fall from the National League pennant to sixth place was probably caused by a little bit of both. Nothing exemplified Pittsburgh's predicament better than the season turned in by 1960 MVP Dick Groat, whose batting average plummeted from a league-leading .325 to .275 and who was even benched for a time for lack of hitting.

But Roberto Clemente was out of sync with the rest of his teammates even in this. Whereas Groat and other key Pirates showed up for the 1961 season fat and comfortable, Clemente came in 10 pounds lighter and with a renewed determination to prove himself. All winter long, he had meditated on the 1960 MVP slight. "I was very bitter," he later admitted. "I am still bitter. I'm a team player. . . . Winning the pennant and the World Championship were more important to me than my average, but I felt I should get the credit I deserved." Clemente had decided—and even promised his parents—that he would channel his anger and resentment into winning the batting title in 1961. This resolution seemed to refresh Clemente, both spiritually and physically. "I'm healthy," he informed the surprised Pittsburgh writers. "I feel real good."

This was bad news for National League pitchers. Clemente bolted out of the starting gate with a flurry of base hits. And he

Clemente amazed baseball people with his unorthodox batting style, which enabled him to stroke inside pitches to the opposite field. Hall of Famer Lou Boudreau called Clemente "one of the worst-looking great hitters I've seen."

seemed to be hitting the ball even more ferociously than ever; it was, as one writer put it, as though the baseballs had "pictures of sportswriters painted on them." Early in the season, Pirates first baseman Dick Stuart watched Clemente take batting practice and observed, "There must be the best 169-pound slugger in baseball." Reserve outfielder Gino Cimoli knew what Stuart meant. On May 9, Cimoli was pitching batting practice when a Clemente line drive struck him in the chest below the heart and sent him to the hospital. Nothing was broken, but Cimoli was out of action until May 21.

In early June, the Pirates were on their way down from second to fourth in the standings, but Clemente's batting average was headed up to .350, following a 15-game streak in which he hit .390. Asked if there was any clubhouse dissension that might be responsible for the team's slump, Danny Murtaugh said, "You'll have to take my word for it, but there isn't any. The only one disgruntled is Roberto, and it hasn't affected his play."

By July, the Pirates were stuck in the middle of the National League standings, and their fans were beginning to give up any hope of a repeat. They now turned their full attention to the efforts of their favorite, Roberto Clemente, to win his first batting title. After all, of the many pleasures of being a baseball fan, few are more satisfying than being able to watch a young player develop day-by-day from a nervous rookie into a star. "As he became greater, they loved him more," said Joe L. Brown. "He proved they were right to have given him their affection. They began saying, 'I knew a long time ago he was great.'" As he continued to excel on the field, Clemente also turned some of his teammates into fans. The same players who had whispered questions about his injuries and called him a prima donna were now kidding him good-naturedly about the 1960 MVP award. Mr. No Votes became his nickname in the Pittsburgh clubhouse.

By midseason, Mr. No Votes was hitting .357 and was about to earn a substitute for the 1960 World Series ring that was gathering dust in his trophy case—a 1961 all-star ring. His first appearance in the All-Star Game was especially gratifying to Clemente because that year the players, coaches, and managers did the voting, instead of the sportswriters or fans. He received 170 votes, second highest on the National League squad and more than the Giants' Willie Mays or Braves slugger Eddie Mathews. When he stepped out onto the field in the company of such greats as Mays, Mathews, Hank Aaron, Frank Robinson, and Ernie Banks, Clemente felt as though he had symbolically arrived to take his place among baseball's first rank of stars. "The players knew I was most valuable last year," Clemente said before the game at San Francisco's Candlestick Park. "Then this year they voted me on the All-Star team. I am feeling very good and I will not let them down."

At Candlestick, neither starting pitcher Whitey Ford nor the rest of the American League staff could handle Clemente. He led off the second inning with a hard triple into right-center field and scored the game's opening run on Bill White's sacrifice fly. In the fourth, Clemente's own sacrifice fly brought home the National League's second run to make the score 2–0. Finally, with the score 4–4 in the bottom of the 10th inning and Willie Mays on second base, Clemente ended the game by cracking a Hoyt Wilhelm knuckleball into right field for a game-winning single.

One hundred games into the season, with the Pirates close to mathematical elimination, Clemente was eliminating his competition from the National League batting race. At .371, he led the nearest hitter by 30 points. He was threatening to lead the Pirates in batting, RBIs, home runs, and runs scored and was making believers all around the country. "Just name me one thing he can't do," asserted Murtaugh. "There's nobody better." Giants third baseman Jim Davenport said, "Clemente has convinced me he's the best hitter in this league. I always thought Hank Aaron was, but Clemente has shown me something. He hits nothing but line drives, and a pitcher never knows where to throw the ball to him."

Clemente finished the season at .351, 8 points higher than runner-up Vada Pinson of the pennant-winning Reds. He had his finest defensive year, recording a career- and league-high 27 assists, and took over Hank Aaron's place as the league's Gold Glove right fielder. He scored 100 runs for the first time in his career and drove in 89. But the most remarkable thing about Clemente's 1961 campaign was his newfound power and consistency. He batted .310 or better against every team in the league—.472 against the Dodgers—and raised his home run total from 16 to 23, with at least one homer in every National League ballpark.

Clemente's ability to bear down with two strikes against him was a major ingredient in his success. Whereas he had once been an easy out when behind in the count, in one game in 1961 Clemente made a remarkable five consecutive base hits on two-strike counts. He also learned how to control his hot temper when pitchers brushed him back or threw at his head. In one game against the Dodgers, Clemente homered off the big right-hander Don Drysdale, who was notorious for terrorizing batters with high, inside pitches. In his next at-bat, a Drysdale fastball sent Clemente sprawling in the dirt. Clemente brushed himself off, stood back in, and whacked another high, inside pitch over the outfield fence. Asked after the game what kind of pitch Clemente had hit, a disgusted Drysdale replied, "Ball four."

Drysdale was not the only first-rate pitcher to be baffled by Clemente's unorthodox hitting style, which contradicted every known rule of hitting technique. Standing at the outer edge of the batter's box and moving into the plate as the pitch was on its way, Clemente should not have been able to handle the inside pitch, but he was. Opening up the left side of his body early in his swing, he should not have been able to cover the outside half of the plate, but he did. Veteran manager Lou Boudreau called him "one of the worst-looking great hitters I've seen. Everything is a line drive." As the great Dodger left-hander Sandy Koufax wrote in his autobiography, "Roberto can hit any pitch, at any time. He will hit pitchouts; he will hit brushback pitches. He will hit high, inside pitches deep to the opposite field, which would be ridiculous even if he didn't do it with both feet off the ground."

Clemente's compatriots celebrated his 1961 batting championship with a triumphant welcome-home party for him and the Giants' Orlando Cepeda, who combined for history's first all–Puerto Rican "Triple Crown." With Cepeda leading the National League in home runs with 46 and in RBIs with 142, Clemente and Cepeda became the first players from Puerto Rico ever to lead either major league in any of the three main batting statistics. Eighteen thousand cheering people greeted the 2 men at the San Juan airport and lined the roads that took their motorcade to the official ceremonies at Sixto Escobar Stadium, which held an additional 5,000 fans.

Thanks to another one of Don Drysdale's calling cards, Clemente needed a second operation on his elbow that winter. But

Clemente is embraced by his mother at San Juan Airport on October 9, 1961, after winning the National League batting title. Orlando Cepeda (facing page), the league leader in home runs and RBIs, also gets a hug from his mother. Eighteen thousand fans showed up to welcome the two stars home.

other than that, the six-year period from 1961 to 1966 was the high point of Clemente's career. He was never healthier or happier. Even though the Pirates as a team continued to flounder, losing Groat, Hoak, and Dick Stuart in a series of disastrous trades after the 1962 season, Clemente elevated his game to a higher level and firmly established himself as one of the finest right fielders ever to play the game. By 1966, the possibility of Roberto Clemente entering the Hall of Fame in Cooperstown, New York, was being discussed for the first time. Every year between 1961 and 1966, he played between 144 and 155 games and batted over .310. He won 3 National League batting titles, with a .339 mark in 1964 and .329 in 1965 to add to his .351 average in 1961, and reached double figures in both outfield assists and home runs in each season. During that period, Clemente won six Gold Glove Awards and played in every All-Star Game. Clemente's 6-year march on baseball posterity was framed neatly by his 1,000th career base hit, a single to right in a game against Cincinnati in August 1961, and his 2,000th in Septem-

ber 1966, a home run into the upper deck at Forbes Field against the Chicago Cubs. As the story goes, when hit number 1,000 rolled into the Reds bullpen, one pitcher observed, "That's Roberto's 1,000th hit." Another asked, "Didn't he get 'em all off of us?"

This was a happy time for Clemente off the field, too. No longer the naive teenager who had flown to Montreal in 1954 or the lonely and misunderstood young man who played in pain through the early days in Pittsburgh, he was a confident major league veteran. One winter day in 1963 when he was in a store back home in Carolina, Clemente set his sights on a new goal. "Who is that pretty young girl?" he asked an acquaintance, as a tall beauty named Vera Cristina Zabala entered the store. It was, according to Vera Zabala, "love at first sight." Not that Clemente said a word to her there in the store; that would have been shockingly forward behavior toward a respectable young woman. It was daring enough for Clemente to find out that she worked in a bank and call her at work. The woman that Clemente had already told his mother he was going to marry refused to take his call.

Eventually, however, some mutual friends arranged a suitable get-together, invited them both, and an old-fashioned Spanish courtship was soon under way. "My family was raised like the old times," Vera Zabala later explained. "We had to ask permission to go from here to the corner." After putting Roberto off for several weeks, she finally agreed to go out on a date, provided they were accompanied by a chaperone.

Clemente soon found out that Vera Zabala knew nothing about baseball and had no idea that he was a famous star. She quickly found out, though, when he visited her at the bank and created a commotion that put a complete stop to the workday. He found her innocence appealing. "I'm going to get married," he told a male friend, adding the following macho sentiment: "I know, I *know*, that she's never been out without a chaperone, and she's never kissed a man in her life. The first guy she's going to kiss is me." Within 9 months, the pair were engaged; within 12 months

Roberto Clemente and Vera Cristina Zabala were married in Carolina, Puerto Rico, in November 1964, in a church ceremony attended by 1,500 people. When the couple first began to date, Zabala knew nothing about baseball and had no idea that Clemente was a celebrity in Puerto Rico.

they were husband and wife. As Vera Clemente remembered, "Everything was so fast!"

The newlyweds moved into an elegant new house in a wealthy section of Río Piedras, after Clemente overcame his initial fears that his old friends from the barrio would be afraid to visit him there. Set on top of a big hill, the Clemente home afforded dramatic views in all directions that included San Juan Bay, the Atlantic Ocean, and distant mountains. Soon, the house was filled with a whole outfield of Clemente boys—Roberto, Jr., Luis, and Enrique—all of whom were born in Puerto Rico at their father's insistence. Clemente, who in the past had never seemed to know what to do with his time away from the diamond, settled into a contented domestic routine. During the time between baseball seasons he played with his sons for hours (although he was never, according to Vera Clemente, able to discipline them) and passed the time by playing the organ, making ceramics, and creating sculptures out of driftwood.

Intense even about his hobbies, Clemente filled room after room with his various creations and made plans to help develop ceramics as a cottage industry in Puerto Rico, in order to help solve the island's chronic unemployment problem. "This is something entire families can do together," he told a friend. "It will unite them." When he traveled with his family, Clemente would avoid tourist attractions and try to get to know how the local people really lived. More often than not, he would come away with a permanent interest in their concerns and problems. This happened on a trip to Nicaragua in the mid-1960s. "When we went to Nicaragua," Vera Clemente remembered, "he said, 'I like it here, because it's like Puerto Rico was before, many years before.' It was country-like, the view and everything, like when they had the sugar plantations in Puerto Rico."

In 1966 the Pirates did not win the pennant, although they stayed in contention until the final week of the season and only missed by three games. Roberto Clemente did not win the batting title or lead the league in any major offensive category. But in many ways, 1966 was Clemente's finest hour. It was the year that he became a true leader in every sense of the word. Without changing his fierce competitiveness or intense pride, Clemente got rid of the chip that had been on his shoulder for a decade and devoted himself completely to his team. He did everything one man could have done to bring another pennant to Pittsburgh and even won over his old enemies, the sportswriters. In a close vote, they named him the National League Most Valuable Player over Sandy Koufax, who had gone 27 and 9 with a 1.73 ERA and pitched the Dodgers to the pennant. "I think he was the MVP because he did so many little

Clemente and Dominican Matty Alou vied for the batting championship in 1966. Although Alou won the title, 1966 was in many ways Clemente's banner year: He drove in 119 runs and was voted Most Valuable Player. Equally important, he became a team leader and even established friendly relations with the press.

things," said Pirates manager Harry Walker, "things that some stars don't do, hustling on routine ground balls, breaking up double plays and hustling to take an extra base. By doing this, he set an example that the others followed and this made him the Most Valuable Player." Catcher Jim Pagliaroni summed up Clemente's influence: "When he speaks in the clubhouse and on the field, everyone respects his word."

Clemente may have mellowed, but he continued to speak out when he saw injustice, using the forum provided by the increased press coverage of the 1966 pennant race. If there was any difference, it was that he spoke more for Hispanics and minorities in general than for himself. "The Latin American player doesn't get the recognition he deserves," Clemente told reporters. "Neither

In the spotlight after his 1966 MVP selection, Clemente took the opportunity to celebrate his Hispanic heritage. He emphasized that the honor given him was most important for its impact on young people in Puerto Rico: "The kids have someone to look to and to follow."

does the Negro player, unless he does something really spectacular, like Willie Mays. We have self-satisfaction, yes. But after the season is over, nobody cares about us. . . . Juan Marichal is one of the greatest pitchers in the game, but does he get invited to banquets? Somebody says we live too far away. That's a lousy excuse. I am an American citizen. But some people act like they think I live in the jungle someplace. To those people, we are outsiders, foreigners."

That winter, when Clemente heard the news at his home that he had become the first Puerto Rican ever to be voted MVP, his reaction combined his usual complete personal candor—he did not deny that he was "expecting it"—with some thoughtful observations on what the honor meant to his country. "When I was a kid I felt that baseball was great to America," he said. "Always, they said Babe Ruth was the best there was . . . but Babe Ruth was an American player. What we needed was a Puerto Rican player they could say that about, someone to look up to and try to equal. Before I came here, you never had many outstanding players from the Caribbean. There were some good ones, like [Orestes "Minnie"] Minoso, but no real outstanding player. I've had many good years. I've won the batting title three times and now I've won the MVP. This makes me happy because now the people feel that if I could do it, then maybe they could do it. The kids have someone to look to and to follow. That's why I like to work with kids so much."

Clemente follows the flight of the ball after whacking a drive to left-center field against the New York Mets on September 30, 1972. Clemente wound up with a double, thus becoming the 11th player in baseball history to achieve 3,000 base hits.

CHAPTER SEVEN

Joining the Immortals

Roberto Clemente had his last MVP-caliber year in 1967, at the age of 33. He won his fourth batting title with a .357 average, swatted 23 home runs, drove in 110 runs, and scored 103. After 1967 he was still the great Clemente, but no longer every day; his tremendous catches, cannonlike throws, and four-hit evenings still came, but they came less often. As his body's resilience declined with age, Clemente was again plagued by injuries to his back, shoulder, and legs. He contended for the batting title in 1969 and 1971, and he was still a perennial all-star and Gold Glove winner in right field. But his dwindling totals in runs scored, RBIs, and games played pointed to the undeniable reality that Clemente was now on the downside of the hill.

The Pirates, on the other hand, were rebuilding. Of the 1960 world champions, only Clemente and Bill Mazeroski were left. The new faces on the team, who turned out to be the foundation of the 1971 champions, included Willie Stargell, Bob Robertson, Al Oliver, Richie Hebner, Gene Alley, Manny Sanguillen, Bob Moose,

Steve Blass, and Dock Ellis. Progress was slow at first, as the Pirates finished sixth in the expanded 10-team National League in both 1967 and 1968. When the National League expanded again and split into the Eastern and Western Divisions in 1969, the Pirates finished third in the East. It was then that the young team jelled and became a major power in baseball, going on to win six division titles and two world championships during the 1970s.

While the Pirates struggled to reestablish themselves, Clemente was building a personal case for baseball immortality. His main goal involved the most basic of all hitting statistics, the base hit. If 1,000 career hits is the mark of an established major league hitter, and 2,000 puts him in the ranks of 200 or so all-stars from a variety of eras, 3,000 hits signifies admission to the ranks of the baseball gods. As of 1967, only 8 men in roughly 100 years of major league play had cracked the magical 3,000-hit barrier—Ty Cobb, Stan Musial, Tris Speaker, Honus Wagner, Eddie Collins, Nap Lajoie, Paul Waner, and Cap Anson. With 2,029 hits going into the 1967 season, Clemente was only a few good years away from joining this select group of Hall of Fame players.

Based on his splendid performance in 1967, when he led the league with 209 hits and raised his total to 2,238, Clemente looked as though he would coast to the 3,000-hit plateau. But his splendid 1967 was followed by a disappointing 1968, due largely to a bad shoulder. Ironically for a player who used his body with such abandon on the playing field, Clemente incurred the injury in February at his home in Río Piedras. The house was built on a wooded hillside, with an extending porch supported by three-inch-thick iron bars. As Clemente was lifting himself up on one of these bars, it gave way. He fell backward, landed hard on his neck, and rolled downhill almost 100 feet. Fortunately, he rolled into a low wall, or he would have gone over the edge of a cliff. A local doctor told him that he had torn a muscle in his shoulder but that everything would be fine with a little rest.

But by the time spring training came, the shoulder was far from healed. Clemente went hitless for 29 straight at-bats and began to worry. "When I swing the bat, I feel weak," he said. By midseason, he was batting only .245 and talking of retirement. Although he acknowledged that his major league salary supported 13 people (his wife and children, his parents, and others, including orphaned nieces and nephews), he explained, "Anytime you're not doing your best, you are stealing the fans' money. And I don't consider myself a thief." Clemente rallied to finish at .291 with 18 home runs, but he was not consoled. "I won't play next year if the shoulder keeps hurting like it does now," he insisted.

The shoulder came around in time for 1969, but in May, Clemente reinjured it making a diving catch. Then he badly tore a thigh muscle slamming into a wall to catch a fly ball against the New York Mets. Finally, after grounding into two double plays in two games and making a costly error in right field, he was booed by the home crowd. This was such unusual treatment for the ever-popular Clemente that one reporter later said, "It took me two minutes to realize they were booing Clemente." Clemente's answer was to tip his hat to the crowd; quickly, the booing turned to laughter and then applause. "I wasn't trying to be smart," he told reporters after the game. "The fans have always been kind to me. When I had trouble with my back in 1956, they were the ones who gave me the lift I needed. And if they figure I have it coming to me now, then they have the right to boo. I was just trying to show them that it was all right with me."

Not long after that, Roberto Clemente turned his season around and played the rest of the year as though he were on a mission. By late June he had raised his batting average from .226 to .314. His improvement was due in large part to the healing of his leg and shoulder, but there were other factors as well. The Pirates were climbing back into contention for the pennant, and Clemente was enjoying the role of providing leadership and a good example for a young, enthusiastic team. "A lot of people don't

Steve Blass was the Pirates' pitching star in the 1971 World Series, winning the third and seventh games while allowing just two earned runs. Blass and Clemente had been teammates since 1964 and enjoyed trading humorous put-downs. "A lot of people don't realize the fun Roberto had," Blass observed.

realize the fun Roberto had, especially in the last five years of his career," said pitcher Steve Blass. Blass and Clemente had a running argument about how they would do if Blass were traded and the two ever faced each other. "I'd throw you inside and take my chances, 'cause I know you're going to hit .350 if I pitch you outside where everybody else does," Blass would say. Clemente would wag his index finger and answer, "Blass, if you pitch me inside, I will hit 43 home runs a year, 37 of them off you!" Third baseman Richie Hebner remembered the tremendous influence exerted by Clemente's work ethic: "Me and some of the other new guys were probably making the minimum, $12,500, and here's Clemente, a guy making $150,000. . . . But when he hits one back to the pitcher he'd run to first like the cops were chasing him!"

By late summer, Clemente's bat was red hot. On August 13, against the Giants, he hit three home runs in his first three at-bats and finished four-for-five. Hitting .335 with a week to go in the season, he had closed to within 11 points of a fifth batting title; New York's Cleon Jones led at .346, and the Reds' Pete Rose was second at .344. Clemente then picked up the pace even more; on the final day of the season, he came within a base hit of taking the lead in the batting race. But Rose had been on a tear of his own, and when the final averages were computed, he edged out Clemente, .348 to .345. However, Clemente led the National League in triples with 10, the last time he would ever lead in a major offensive category.

As the 1970 season began, Clemente announced to reporters that 3,000 hits were within sight: "I need 441 hits to reach the 3,000 mark for my career. If nothing happens to me, I can do it. In fact,

Clemente robs the Mets' Cleon Jones of an extra-base hit during a game at New York's Shea Stadium. The winner of a dozen Gold Glove Awards as the National League's best right fielder, Clemente dazzled the fans with spectacular running catches and bulletlike throws.

I could play four more years if I feel like I do right now." On August 22 and 23, in the heat of a tight pennant race, Clemente collected 10 of his needed hits against his favorite opponent, the Dodgers, in Los Angeles. The first game was a 4½-hour pitchers' duel that was won by Pittsburgh 2–1 in the 16th inning when Clemente reached base via his fifth hit, stole second, and scored the winning run; he had driven in the Pirates' only other run with a single in the third. The game had ended at midnight, and the following afternoon, after a very short night's sleep, the 36-year-old Clemente drove in 3 runs and scored 4 as he banged out 3 singles, a double, and a home run in an 11–0 Pittsburgh rout. No other major leaguer since 1900 had ever recorded 10 hits in 2 consecutive games. An awed Danny Murtaugh said, "Man, when I was playing, it would take me three or four weeks to get that many hits." The pair of victories increased the Pirates' lead over second-place New York to three games; they never looked back and went on to finish first by five games.

Murtaugh made judicious use of his star right fielder over the next two seasons, giving him lots of rest, and the Pirates won two more division titles. In 1971, the Pirates also won the pennant and defeated the Baltimore Orioles in a thrilling, seven-game World Series. Due to his MVP performance in the series, Clemente finally got the national recognition his talents deserved. But his goal of 3,000 hits was still in the distance. Even though he had batted .352 and .341 in 1970 and 1971, he had averaged only 120 games played; with only 145 and 178 hits in each season, Clemente was 118 hits short as the curtain went up on the 1972 season.

He was also hurting. That spring, he had made his annual announcement that he would only play one or two more seasons. "There is no way I will play after 1973," he insisted. This time, he may have meant it. A bad ankle and severely bruised heels took him out of the lineup for 47 of the Pirates' first 116 games. Stomach trouble and general physical exhaustion made him lose so much weight that he had to borrow a pair of uniform pants from Rennie

Clemente became the Pirates' all-time RBI leader when he broke Pie Traynor's record (1,273) on June 20, 1972. He was proud of the record but refused to tip his cap when the fans gave him a standing ovation during the game: This was his way of honoring Traynor, a Hall of Fame third baseman who had died in Pittsburgh just three months earlier.

Stennett, the slender second baseman. He limped past milestones such as Pie Traynor's Pirates RBI record of 1,273. (Upon breaking this record he refused to acknowledge the fans' standing ovation and later explained, "The man whose record I broke was a great ballplayer, a great fellow. And he just died here a few months ago. That's why I didn't tip my cap.") Then he surpassed Honus Wagner's Pirates career hit record of 2,971. He entered the month of September needing 25 hits to reach 3,000.

With the Pirates holding a comfortable 15-game lead in the Eastern Division, the spotlight focused squarely on Clemente's personal race for 3,000. He responded by raising his batting average into the .310s. Throughout the month of September, Clemente chipped away at the record, base hit by base hit. On September 27, he got 2 hits in Philadelphia to give him 2,998; on September 28, he collected number 2,999 off the Phillies' great lefty Steve Carlton. The next night, the Pirates returned to Pittsburgh and were welcomed by 24,000 fans eager to see Clemente make history against the New York Mets and their ace, Tom Seaver. In the first inning, Clemente hit a high bouncer over the pitcher's mound that glanced off second baseman Ken Boswell's glove and rolled into center field. Clemente waited at first base, not knowing whether the official scorer had ruled it a hit or an error. The crowd cheered when the scoreboard flashed an *H*, for "hit." But then, as the baseball was being retrieved for Clemente, the board flashed an *E*, for "error." There had been a misunderstanding between the official scorer and the scoreboard operator. The happy fans turned angry and let out a torrent of boos. They went home even more disappointed after Clemente finished the night without a hit.

Back in the Pittsburgh locker room after the game, Clemente was boiling mad. After a few hours, however, he settled down and conceded, "I'm glad they didn't call it a hit. I want to get it without

Clemente had a tremendous following in New York, which has a large Puerto Rican population. In September 1971, the Mets staged a Roberto Clemente Night at Shea Stadium. Clemente attended with his parents, his wife, and his three sons, Luis, Roberto, Jr., and Enrique.

Umpire Doug Harvey hands Clemente the ball that he stroked for his historic 3,000th hit. The game was held up for a full minute while the fans stood and cheered the star outfielder. Neither he nor they had any idea that the hit would be his last.

taint." And the next afternoon, at precisely 3:07 P.M., Clemente stepped up to the plate and whacked a Jon Matlack curveball off the wall in left-center for a double—his 3,000th career base hit. There was no doubt about this one, and it was fitting that in this moment of glory Clemente should be standing in the middle of the wide, green baseball field, all alone. As Matlack graciously delayed the game by refusing to take the mound for a full minute, umpire Doug Harvey handed Clemente the baseball he had hit and offered his congratulations.

The fans cheered and cheered for Clemente, who now joined Willie Mays and Hank Aaron (who had both reached 3,000 in 1970) and the other 8 immortals in the 3,000-hit club. Clemente kept one foot on second base and waved to the crowd with his batting helmet. His old Santurce teammate Willie Mays jogged out from the visitors' dugout to shake his hand. "I give this hit," Clemente said after the game, "to the fans of Pittsburgh and to the people of Puerto Rico and the man who made me play baseball, Roberto Marín."

Pittsburgh coach Frank Oceak congratulates Clemente after his home run in Game 7 of the 1971 World Series. After dominating the series, Clemente was a sought-after guest on TV talk shows, where he displayed the dignity and sincerity that had made him a national hero in Puerto Rico.

CHAPTER EIGHT

"Clemente Has Always Been There"

After getting his 3,000th hit, Clemente did not play any more games in the 1972 regular season. The Pirates were not trying to be dramatic; they wanted their big hitter to get some rest before the pennant playoffs against the Cincinnati Reds. No one could have known that by New Year's Day, 1973, Clemente would be dead and that hit number 3,000 would turn out to be his last.

After the playoffs, won by the Reds, three games to two, Clemente returned home, as usual, for the holiday season, which in Puerto Rico is celebrated with several weeks of parties, feasts, and spontaneous get-togethers among friends and family. All this was in full swing when Clemente heard some bad news from Nicaragua. On December 23, 1972, a severe earthquake destroyed much of the capital city of Managua, killing and injuring thousands of people and driving many more from their homes. Before the day was over, Clemente had already volunteered to serve as chairman of the Puerto Rican chapter of the Nicaraguan relief effort and had thrown himself into the job. Whereas to most celebrities such a title would signify nothing more than a way of lending a famous name, Clemente personally and tirelessly enlisted friends and strangers to send money, food, clothing, and supplies to the victims. For the week following the disaster, he worked around the clock; at one point he even walked from door to door in his Río Piedras neighborhood to ask for donations. "He forgot all about eating," remembered a friend who visited him on Christmas Day. "About two in the afternoon, I asked him if he'd eaten, and he said he'd had a small piece of *morcilla* [a type of sausage]. I asked him to come to the house for lunch; we lived nearby, but he said, 'No, just bring me a little coffee.'"

By December 31, Clemente's relief organization had collected enough supplies to fill a rickety old DC-7 cargo plane that had been donated by a San Juan company. The plane was scheduled to take off for Nicaragua in the afternoon, and Clemente was planning to be on it. As the flight was repeatedly delayed by small mechanical problems, a number of friends, as well as his wife, urged Clemente not to make the trip. "Babies are dying there," was his answer. "They need these supplies."

There were two other things on Clemente's mind that evening. One was a young orphan boy that he had met in a Managua hospital the previous November, when Clemente was managing a Puerto Rican amateur team in an international tournament. The boy needed a pair of artificial legs, and Clemente and other members of the team had contributed the money to pay for them; now, Clemente was worried that the boy might not have survived. His other concern stemmed from a phone call he had received from General Anastasio Somoza, the dictator of Nicaragua, in which Somoza told Clemente that he would only accept "money and food" from the relief effort. For Clemente, this confirmed rumors that Somoza's army was keeping the donations for itself. There was only one way to prevent this; they would never have the nerve to steal relief supplies in the presence of an international hero such as Clemente. "I'll go down and distribute the supplies myself," he declared.

Shortly after 9:00 P.M. the DC-7 finally took off, carrying Roberto Clemente and four others. They never arrived in Nicaragua. The plane developed engine trouble during takeoff and rapidly lost speed; pilot Jerry Hill radioed the control tower that he was going to return to San Juan. Witnesses saw the plane bank hard to the left and then fall into the sea. No survivors were spotted. Three hours later, Vera Clemente got a call from her niece, telling her what had happened. "Oh no," she said, "it's not possible. He is in Nicaragua."

The shock of Roberto Clemente's death extended to Pittsburgh, where his teammates' New Year's Eve parties turned into wakes, and across the baseball world. What made it even harder for many to accept was that Clemente's body was never found. When dawn broke on the first day of 1973, thousands of Puerto Ricans were gathered silently along the beach near where the plane had gone down; some waded into the water as though hoping to find some sign of their dead hero. The Coast Guard searched for days. They found the remains of the pilot, but not Clemente—only a few of his possessions, including a sock and a small, empty suitcase. His old friend and teammate Manny Sanguillen put on scuba gear and conducted his own personal search. "I went down in the water for the last time five days after the crash," he later

Luisa and Melchor Clemente are comforted by friends as they wait for news of their son, shortly after his plane crashed in the Caribbean Sea on New Year's Eve, 1972. Clemente had insisted on bringing supplies to Nicaragua's earthquake victims in person, despite warnings that the plane was unsafe.

recalled, "when they said they saw a body. It was only a green fish. I also saw this big shark. I saw a lot of sharks down there before. This one was really big. It did not scare me, but only made me sad . . . very sad."

Clemente's fans in both Pittsburgh and Puerto Rico came together on January 4 to mourn his death with a joint mass that was held simultaneously in a church in downtown Pittsburgh and in Carolina's San Fernando Church, where Clemente had been baptized and married. Baseball Commissioner Bowie Kuhn, Pirates president Dan Galbreath, and the entire Pirates team flew down to Clemente's hometown and grieved along with thousands of his friends and neighbors. The inauguration of Rafael Hernández Colón, the island's new governor, was postponed for four days; when it was finally held, it was more of a memorial service for Clemente than a postelection celebration. "Our people," Colón said, "have lost one of their great glories."

On March 20, 1973, the baseball writers voted Roberto Clemente the unprecedented honor of immediate induction into the Hall of Fame, without the usual waiting period of five years after a player's last game. On April 5, the Pittsburgh Pirates retired Clemente's number 21 and, in a ceremony at home plate in Three Rivers Stadium, handed over his jersey to Vera and Luisa Clemente. For months afterward, Vera Clemente said, "I would receive a big package of mail, letters from all over the world. I knew from travelling that everyone loved him. When I received all that mail, I knew how far it went."

Roberto Clemente left a legacy that transcended the baseball diamond. The imprint of his life can still be seen not only in baseball box scores but also in the hearts of the many young people that he touched in one way or another. Throughout his career, he gave hours and hours of his time to instructing aspiring ballplayers. "You should learn the fundamentals," he told them. "Work on them. Keep out of trouble. Don't do anything your dear ones will be ashamed of. This is a great game. It can do a lot for you, but only if you give it all you can. Now, go and hit one for me." When an older Puerto Rican boy showed some promise of becoming a major leaguer, Clemente would often take him under his wing and give him the kind of guidance that Clemente never got when he was a teenage prospect. Outfielder Willie Montanez was one player that Clemente helped; another was pitcher John Candelaria, who remembered, "The first Pirate I met when they were trying to sign me was Clemente. Clemente was supposed to be arguing for the front office. But while they tried to talk me into signing, Clemente kept telling me in Spanish: 'You can get more money.'"

Roberto Clemente's death spurred an outpouring of donations to Ciudad Deportiva, or Sports City, a project that Clemente had been struggling to get off the ground in San Juan for years. He had envisioned a sports facility that would provide recreation for poor children; he called it "the biggest ambition in my life." According to a friend, Clemente believed that "sports was one of the best ways to imbue in youth the values of good citizenship. . . . He felt that with sports the child learned in a natural way, at an important stage in life, that one must sacrifice a bit for the common good." Today, thanks to donations from governments, corporations, major league baseball, and private citizens from Puerto Rico and the rest of the United States, Sports City is a reality. One of its graduates is Texas Rangers star Ruben Sierra, who, along with veteran Philadelphia Phillies shortstop Dickie Thon, pays tribute to Roberto Clemente by wearing the number 21 on his back. Sports City is only one of many places where the memory of Clemente's love for young people is kept alive. From San Juan to Pittsburgh to New York, millions of children have attended schools dedicated to Clemente and played in parks or on ball fields bearing his name.

Roberto Clemente also occupies a very large space in the baseball record books. He won 4 batting titles and batted over .300 in 13 out of 18 seasons. He hit .362 lifetime in the World Series and .323 in All-Star Games. He won a dozen Gold Glove Awards and played on an equal number of National League all-star teams. He won the MVP Award once and finished in the top 10 in the voting 7 times. On a team that has featured such baseball immortals as Honus Wagner, Fred Clarke, Pie Traynor, Paul Waner, Max Carey, Kiki Cuyler, Arky Vaughan, Ralph Kiner, and Willie Stargell, Roberto Clemente is the all-time leader in career games, at-bats, hits, singles, and total bases. His career spanned one of the worst eras for batting average in modern history; in 1968, for example, Carl Yastrzemski of the Boston Red Sox led the American League with a batting average of only .301. Yet Clemente compiled a lifetime batting average of .317 and batted over .320 in 8 seasons. He played in a home park that discouraged the long ball but still hit 240 home runs; realizing that it would be futile to try for the fences all the time, Clemente used his power to hit the ball in the gaps and used his speed to leg out triples. He reached double figures in triples in 9 seasons and finished with a total of 166. Playing at a time when the stolen base was out of fashion, Clemente stole only 83 bases in his career. In a different time or place, Clemente could have been a great base stealer, or a great power hitter, or both.

Roberto Clemente always had a special relationship with the fans, completely unaffected by his differences with the press. In both Pittsburgh and San Juan, he frequently found that he could not pay for a meal or something else that he tried to buy. Clemente once argued and argued with a shop owner who refused to take his money, until the man finally explained that when he had been a young boy and sitting in the right field stands at Forbes Field, an older fan outwrestled him for a foul ball that had landed nearby. The following inning, Clemente had gone over and given him another ball "for the one they took away from you." The shop owner concluded, "That's why I can't charge you." When the Pittsburgh fans held a Roberto Clemente Night in 1970, they were joined by a delegation from Puerto Rico that presented Clemente with a number of gifts, including a scroll bearing 300,000 signatures of his fellow Puerto Ricans. After the game, Clemente cried and said, "If it wasn't for these fans, I don't know what would have happened to me."

Clemente had a rare sense of responsibility to the people who

A tearful Vera Clemente accepts her husband's 1972 Gold Glove Award on opening day of the 1973 season. In a special ceremony at home plate, the Pirates paid tribute to Roberto Clemente and announced that no other Pirate would ever wear number 21. "A country without idols is nothing," Clemente once said.

truly paid his salary. "A country without idols is nothing," he once said. "I send out 20,000 autographed pictures a year to the kids. I feel proud when a kid asks me for my autograph. I do it because baseball has given me a good life. . . . Some players complain. I tell them that we do not have to stand in the street with a heavy drill going rat-tat-tat. . . . I believe we owe something to the people who watch us. They work hard for their money."

And above all, Roberto Clemente left behind the memory of the fierce, all-out style with which he played the game of baseball. Neither his fans nor his fellow players will ever forget the line drives that rocketed off his bat into the right-field gap; his bullet throws that cut down so many enemy base runners; and above all, the complete dedication to his craft that made his brilliant feats possible. After Clemente's death, one teammate told of having gone to the ballpark on the day of a rainout and discovering Clemente, alone in the outfield, practicing a new grip that would enable him to make long, accurate throws with a wet baseball. Another said: "Sometime this year, somebody is going to go from first to third against us on a single to right. And I'm going to be shocked. It's never happened before, in all the time I've been in the big leagues, because Clemente has always been there."

Career Statistics

Year	G	AB	R	H	2B	3B	HR	RBI	SB	AVG
1955	124	474	48	121	23	11	5	47	2	.255
1956	147	543	66	169	30	7	7	60	6	.311
1957	111	451	42	114	17	7	4	30	0	.253
1958	140	519	69	150	24	10	6	50	8	.289
1959	105	432	60	128	17	7	4	50	2	.296
1960	144	570	89	179	22	6	16	94	4	.314
1961	146	572	100	201	30	10	23	89	4	.351
1962	144	538	95	168	28	9	10	74	6	.312
1963	152	600	77	192	23	8	17	76	12	.320
1964	155	622	95	211	40	7	12	87	5	.339
1965	152	589	91	194	21	14	10	65	8	.329
1966	154	638	105	202	31	11	29	119	7	.317
1967	147	585	103	209	26	10	23	110	9	.357
1968	132	502	74	146	18	12	18	57	2	.291
1969	138	507	87	175	20	12	19	91	4	.345
1970	108	412	65	145	22	10	14	60	3	.352
1971	132	522	82	178	29	8	13	86	1	.341
1972	102	378	68	118	19	7	10	60	0	.312
18 yrs.	2,433	9,454	1,416	3,000	440	166	240	1,305	83	.317

Chronology

1934	Born Roberto Walker Clemente on August 18 in Carolina, Puerto Rico
1947	Jackie Robinson joins the Brooklyn Dodgers and becomes the first black player in the major leagues
1948	Clemente discovered by Roberto Marín
1952	Signs first professional contract with the Santurce Cangrejeros of the Puerto Rican League
1954	Signed by the Brooklyn Dodgers in February and assigned to Triple-A Montreal Royals; purchased by the Pittsburgh Pirates in November for $4,000 draft price
1955	In April, singles against Brooklyn in first major league at-bat
1958	Leads all National League outfielders in assists (22) for the first of 5 seasons; hits 3 triples in 1 game to tie major league record
1960	Finishes a disappointing eighth in the MVP voting; Pirates win World Series in seven games over the New York Yankees

1961	Clemente records 1,000th career base hit and wins first batting title with .351 average; wins first of 12 Gold Gloves and appears in first All-Star Game
1963	Suspended for five days for striking an umpire
1964	Marries Vera Cristina Zabala; wins second batting title
1965	Contracts malaria before spring training; wins third batting title
1966	Records 2,000th base hit; becomes first Puerto Rican baseball player to win the MVP Award
1967	Wins fourth and final batting title with a .357 average
1968	Seriously injures shoulder in fall
1970	Collects 10 hits in 2 days against the Los Angeles Dodgers; honored at Three Rivers Stadium in Pittsburgh with Roberto Clemente Night; severely strains back in September
1971	Bats .414 in World Series against the Baltimore Orioles and is named Series MVP
1972	Records 3,000th base hit in his last professional appearance, on September 30; killed in plane crash on New Year's Eve
1973	Clemente's number 21 is retired by the Pirates; Clemente becomes first Hispanic player ever to be voted into the Hall of Fame

Further Reading

Brondfield, Jerry. *Roberto Clemente: Pride of the Pirates*. Champaign, IL: Garrard, 1976.

Cepeda, Orlando, and Charles Einstein. *My Ups and Downs in Baseball*. New York: Putnam, 1968.

Christine, Bill. *Roberto!* New York: Stadia Sports, 1973.

Gerber, Irving. *Roberto Clemente: The Pride of Puerto Rico*. North Bergen, NJ: Book-Lab, 1978.

James, Bill. *The Bill James Historical Abstract*. New York: Villard Books, 1988.

Miller, Ira, and Jose M. Perez. *Roberto Clemente*. New York: Grosset & Dunlap, 1973.

Musick, Phil. *Who Was Roberto?* Garden City, NY: Doubleday, 1974.

Peterson, Robert. *Only the Ball Was White*. Englewood Cliffs, NJ: Prentice-Hall, 1970.

Rodriguez-Mayoral, Luis. *Roberto Clemente: Aún Escucha las Ovaciones*. Carolina, Puerto Rico: Ciudad Deportiva Roberto Clemente, 1987.

Smith, Robert. *Illustrated History of Baseball.* New York: Grosset & Dunlap, 1973.

Smizik, Bob. *The Pittsburgh Pirates: An Illustrated History.* New York: Walker, 1990.

Stargell, Willie, and Tom Bird. *Willie Stargell: An Autobiography.* New York: HarperCollins, 1984.

Thorn, John, and Pete Palmer, eds. *Total Baseball.* New York: Warner, 1989.

Tygiel, Jules. *Baseball's Great Experiment: Jackie Robinson and His Legacy.* New York: Oxford University Press, 1983.

Wagenheim, Kal. *Clemente!* New York: Praeger, 1973.

Index

THOMAS W. GILBERT holds a degree in classics from Yale University. A former dictionary and textbook editor, he is the principal author of *150 Years of Baseball*, a history of the national pastime from its early days to the present, and coauthor of two other books on baseball. He is a frequent contributor to many national publications.

RODOLFO CARDONA is professor of Spanish and comparative literature at Boston University. A renowned scholar, he has written many works of criticism, including *Ramón, a Study of Gómez de la Serna and His Works* and *Visión del esperpento: Teoría y práctica del esperpento en Valle-Inclán*. Born in San José, Costa Rica, he earned his B.A. and M.A. from Louisiana State University and received a Ph.D. from the University of Washington. He has taught at Case Western Reserve University, the University of Pittsburgh, the University of Texas at Austin, the University of New Mexico, and Harvard University.

JAMES COCKCROFT is currently a visiting professor of Latin American and Caribbean studies at the State University of New York at Albany. A three-time Fulbright scholar, he earned a Ph.D. from Stanford University and has taught at the University of Massachusetts, the University of Vermont, and the University of Connecticut. He is the author or coauthor of numerous books on Latin American subjects, including *Neighbors in Turmoil: Latin America*, *The Hispanic Experience in the United States: Contemporary Issues and Perspectives*, and *Outlaws in the Promised Land: Mexican Immigrant Workers and America's Future*.